# how to *feed* yourself

## recipes for real life from a young & hungry foodie

# how to *feed* yourself

recipes for real life from a young & hungry foodie

Becky Duffett

photos by Matt Schriock

# contents

6    intro

8    setting up the kitchen

9    stocking the pantry

10   fresh flavors

11   tips & tricks


13   chapter 1: veggie-riffic  *veggies & beans*

33   chapter 2: cheap carbs  *pasta, pizza & grains*

57   chapter 3: fish delish  *fish & shellfish*

77   chapter 4: winner chicken dinner  *chicken & turkey*

97   chapter 5: extra meaty  *beef, pork & lamb*

119  chapter 6: party food  *snacks, dinner, bbq & brunch*

149  chapter 7: guilty pleasures  *sweets & snacks*


170  index

When I graduated from college, my first real job was at a cookbook publisher. My friends were excited about this. They asked a lot of questions, like, "When can I come over for dinner?" and "Do you have any cookbook recommendations?"

The second question was harder to answer. I wanted to say, "Get the Joy of Cooking!" which was my first cookbook love. But I knew that a tome would sit on the shelf, unapproachable and unopened. I thought about fun, flashy cookbooks from trending restaurants and bloggers. But I knew that those too would disappoint. My friends would try a recipe or two, despair that they didn't own a sous vide, buy a bunch of ingredients they'd never use again, and then give up at the first mention of spatchcocking a chicken.

Don't get me wrong, my friends are smart kids, grads who could research an obscure topic, write a persuasive paper, and solve complex problem sets. I have complete faith that every last one of them could chop an onion, or at least figure it out. Yet they still lived on takeout burritos and frozen dinners from Trader Joe's.

Sound familiar? Whether you're fresh out of college, leaning into your career in your 20s, or at any other age and stage of your life and looking for more inspiration in the kitchen, this book is for you.

This is my collection of go-to recipes—the recipes I recommend to my friends, because they're simple, straightforward, and satisfying. They're from scratch but not scary. I wrote a hundred of them, because I appreciate good value and know you do, too. I avoided expensive ingredients and fancy equipment. I focused on easy weeknight dinners, but I threw in some party food (page 119) and sweets and snacks (page 149), to cover other occasions and cravings.

Like many young foodies, I eat a whole lot of everything, and my style is a mix of comfort food and fresh flavors. My recipes draw inspiration from '80s and '90s kids' throwbacks (baked mac and cheese with garlicky crumbs, page 46), takeout replacements (Sriracha fried rice with sunny eggs, page 42), food trucks (fish tacos with pickled onions, page 66), and other fun, fresh ideas (crispy treat hacks and popcorn remixes, pages 154 and 129).

Feeding yourself is a basic life skill, but eating well and nourishing the people you love is an undiluted pleasure. I hope you find some favorite recipes, work them into your weekly routine, and crank up the tunes in the kitchen.

♡, Becky

# setting up the kitchen

*If you're setting up your kitchen, here are some guidelines. Some tools are fine to buy on the cheap, others are worth investing in. Avoid knife blocks with sixteen flimsy blades, massive cookware sets with everything in the same material, and low-quality nonstick pans. Do splurge on a few decent knives, a stainless-steel sauté pan, and a cast-iron Dutch oven. Personally, I go low budget on cutting boards, bowls, and baking sheets.*

## knives

Paring knife (for trimming vegetables)

Serrated knife (for slicing bread)

Chef's knife (for chopping)

## pots & pans

Small stainless-steel saucepan
(with sloped sides for whisking)

Large stainless-steel sauté pan
(with straight sides and a lid for simmering)

Large cast-iron skillet

Large nonstick frying pan

Enameled cast-iron Dutch oven

Small pot (for steaming vegetables)

Large pot (for boiling pasta)

Colander (for draining)

## bakeware

8-by-8-inch (20-by-20-cm) baking pan

9-by-13-inch (23-by-33-cm) baking pan

2 large rimmed baking sheets

Two 9-inch (23-cm) round cake pans

5-by-9-inch (13-by-23-cm) loaf pan

Standard 12-cup muffin pan

## bowls

4 small ramekins (prep bowls)

Small, medium, and large mixing bowls

## boards

Small cutting board
(for garlic, onion, herbs)

Large cutting board
(for rolling out dough)

## tools

Nested measuring cups
(for dry ingredients)

2-cup (16-fl-oz/500-ml) glass
measuring cup (for wet ingredients)

Measuring spoons

Pastry brush

Silicon spatula

Metal spatula

Wooden spoons

Kitchen tongs

Serving spoons

Can opener

Pepper grinder

Box grater-shredder

Wine opener

Bottle opener

## electrics

Blender

Food processor

Stand mixer

## tabletop

4 large plates

4 small plates

4 soup bowls

8 forks, knives, and spoons

4 drinking glasses

4 wineglasses

4 mugs

## linens

Apron

Oven mitts

Napkins

Tea towels

Tablecloth

## serving

Tray

Large serving platter

Wide serving bowl

# stocking the pantry

Some staples are always nice to have on hand. You'll still need to shop for fresh ingredients and recipe specifics, but this is a good start. For herbs and spices, avoid prefab mixes or sets. Better to build a library based on your favorite recipes and flavors. Refresh after 6 months or when the aroma starts to fade.

## salt & pepper

Kosher salt (see note)

Black peppercorns

Ground white pepper

## dried herbs & spices

Basil

Bay leaves

Dill weed

Oregano

Rosemary

Thyme

Cayenne pepper

Chile powder

Coriander

Cumin

Paprika

Red pepper flakes

Allspice

Cinnamon

Cloves

Ginger

Nutmeg

## pantry staples

Olive oil (see note)

Canola or vegetable oil

Vinegars (balsamic, red, white)

Worcestershire sauce

Rice

Pasta

Beans

Yellow onions

Garlic

Fresh ginger

Breadcrumbs

Canned tomatoes

Tomato paste

Dijon mustard

Capers

## baking essentials

All-purpose flour

Rolled oats

Granulated sugar

Brown sugar

Confectioners' sugar

Unsweetened cocoa powder

Baking powder

Baking soda

Pure vanilla extract

Chocolate chips

Walnuts

## fridge & freezer

Unsalted butter

Large eggs

Milk

Stock (veggie, chicken, beef)

Frozen puff pastry

Frozen peas

A note on kosher salt: **All of the recipes in this book were tested with kosher salt, which has large, mild flakes. If you use sea salt or standard table salt, scale back on quantities. For garnish, pick up a box of Spanish Maldon. Sprinkle the big, beautiful flakes over a gorgeous steak (page 99) or sticky-sweet dessert (page 146).**

A note on olive oil: **Extra-virgin olive oil is everywhere these days. Technically, regular is best for sautéing and roasting, and extra-virgin is best for drizzling and dressing. It's kind of a shame to heat up extra-virgin and lose those extra-pure, expensive flavors. But truthfully, my grocery store carries only extra-virgin. It's a marketing ploy, which I am currently funding, because I use it on everything.**

# fresh flavors

*These days, many grocery stores stock ingredients from all over the world. Look for these fresh flavors on the international aisle, or explore ethnic groceries for specialty items. Of course, there's always Amazon.*

## asian flavors

mirin: A sweet Japanese rice wine, which adds subtle flavor to stir-fries and marinades.

oyster sauce: A dark, thick sauce made from oysters. In Cantonese and Southeast Asian cooking, it often flavors noodles or meat.

hoisin sauce: A thick and pungent condiment, made from starches, garlic, and chile. In Cantonese cooking, it's often used as a glaze or dipping sauce.

rice vinegar: Similar to Western wine vinegars, but with a clean, bright flavor.

sriracha sauce: The popular bright red chile sauce, with a rooster on the bottle. Originally from Thailand and Vietnam. Drizzle it over soups, noodles, rice, or almost anything.

soy sauce: The staple salty seasoning from China and Japan. Types range from dark to light and low-sodium options.

sesame oil: A natural oil with delicate aroma and flavor. Most varieties start to smoke at high heat, and are reserved for drizzling and finishing a dish, rather than cooking.

wasabi paste: The green and fiery Japanese condiment, often compared to horseradish. It comes premade in small tubes.

sesame seeds: Black or white sesame seeds are a pretty, lightly crunchy garnish.

## thai flavors

coconut milk: A staple of Southeast Asian cooking, make sure to buy coconut milk, not cream, and shake before you open. It's full of healthy fats, but there are light options, if you prefer.

red curry paste: A blend of red chiles, lemongrass, and galangal. Stir a spoonful into coconut milk to make a simmer sauce for chicken, duck, or beef.

green curry paste: A blend of green chiles, lemongrass, and galangal. Combine with coconut milk and simmer veggies, prawns, or chicken.

lemongrass: A fresh herb that adds lemony aroma to curries. Crush the stalk to release the flavor, but leave it whole, so you can remove and discard. It's too tough to eat.

fish sauce: The staple salty seasoning from Thailand, made from fermented fish. You can substitute soy sauce, although they do have different flavors.

thai basil: A fresh herb, similar to sweet basil, but with smaller leaves, purple stems, and distinctive licorice flavor.

## latin flavors

crema: A tangy cultured cream, like sour cream but runnier.

fresh chiles: Chiles range in heat from mellow poblanos to medium jalapeños to fiery habaneros. Most of the heat comes from the ribs and seeds, remove to tone them down. Wash hands carefully after handling, or wear gloves for the hottest.

chile powders: Look for pure chile powders made from ground ancho, pasilla, or cayenne peppers. "Chili" powder is often a blend with cumin and other spices.

chipotle chiles in adobo sauce: Chipotle chiles are jalapeños that have been dried and smoked, resulting in big flavor. Look for them canned in adobo sauce or in powder form.

mole poblano: There are several types of mole sauces, but poblano is iconic. A long list of ingredients, including chiles and chocolate, is blended into a dark, savory sauce. Look for premade cans or boxes, such as Doña María.

queso fresco: The fresh farmer's cheese, with light, creamy flavor. Crumble and serve over mole, enchiladas, or salad.

salsa fresca: Also called pico de gallo. An uncooked combination of finely chopped vegetables, including tomato, chile, onion, and cilantro. It's usually mild.

## indian spices

turmeric: Cumin and coriander are the basis of many curries, but vibrant yellow turmeric adds another depth of earthy flavor.

fenugreek seeds: The dried seeds of a plant, which resemble little golden pebbles. A fraction of a teaspoon adds nutty, golden flavor.

cardamom: Whole cardamom pods have a distinctive flavor and aroma, bright and clean, open to sweet or savory. Add to curries or rice during cooking, but remove before serving.

# tips & tricks

## how much to buy

Whenever my brother Jason calls, there's a pretty good chance that he's standing in front of the meat counter, because he decided to host a barbecue and has no idea how much brisket to buy. It depends on how hungry your friends are and what else you're cooking, but here are some guidelines to help you estimate. Measures are per person.

$1/4$ **lb boneless, skinless chicken breasts or lean meat**

$1/3$ **lb fish fillet**

$1/2$ **lb bone-in chicken or meat**

$1/2$ **lb stew meat**

$1/8$ **lb dried pasta**

$1/4$ **cup uncooked rice**

## shop fresh, local, seasonal

It's a cliché, but it simply tastes better. Don't set your heart on a recipe, go to the store, and resign yourself to buying something sad, frozen, or from a far-off continent. Tender asparagus, peas, and baby greens are best in spring. Heat-hungry tomatoes, zucchini, and eggplant thrive in summer. Sturdy root vegetables and orange-fleshed squashes sweeten in crisp autumn. Check out what looks good at the farmers' market, and keep that in mind.

## taste as you go

Make sure you're tasting and adjusting during cooking. I like what I like, but you like what you like, and recipes still work if you amp up a spice, use a different green herb, or drop the garlic. Even if you're the kind of person who diligently follows recipes, always taste for salt. With kosher salt, I find that 1 teaspoon per pound of meat or chicken is a safe rule. Scale back if you're using table salt. But keep an eye out for other salty ingredients, like stock, Parmesan, and capers, and balance accordingly.

## find your rhythm

Experienced cooks develop an innate sense of timing. Every oven, stove, pan, and cook is different. I gave approximate cook times in this book, but at the end of the day, it's you in the kitchen. Watch for golden edges and surfaces. Listen to how fast the bubbles are rising or the oil is sizzling. Smell what's happening to that pan of brownies. Good cooks don't use clocks, they rely on their senses. You may not be there yet, but the best advice I have is to be observant and learn from experience.

## don't prod meat

Every time you nudge, turn, or otherwise touch that steak or chicken breast, you're toughening it. Trust yourself. Let it sit, brown, go crusty at the edges, and turn delicious. Gently press to see if it's firm (cooked) or still gives (pink at the center).

## don't overcook veggies

My boyfriend is British, and he is the worst at this. Onions are the one exception—there are times when you'll want them to sink, soften, and caramelize. But green vegetables are usually at their best when brightly colored and crisp to the bite. For tender beans and peas, that can be a scant minute or two. For broccoli and sturdier specimens, it might be a few. For spinach and cooking greens, just watch until they start to sink, and then pull them off the heat.

## don't panic

If your onions are overbrowning and you're not ready with the next ingredient—pull your pan off the burner for a minute. If a soup or a salad dressing isn't tasting right, experiment with some different seasonings. Cooking is a process, and most recipes are forgiving. Give yourself a break, and don't give up too soon.

## google, youtube, and the blogosphere

This book assumes that you've done a little bit of cooking prep work—or at least, you have a valid internet connection. If you really don't know how to chop an onion, peel a clove of garlic, toast nuts, or properly measure flour—never fear! I promise you, there is a cooking blogger who has written a step-by-step or made a video tutorial. The web is a wide, wonderful place, with many answers.

# chapter 1: veggie-riffic
## veggies & beans

15    massaged kale salad with dates & nuts

16    butternut squash soup with fried sage

18    creamy tomato soup & onion toasties

19    wild mushroom stew with dill & paprika

21    three amigos bean chili

22    asparagus & baby shiitake stir-fry

24    eggplant parm

25    co-op quesadillas with beets & chard

27    jacket potatoes with fillings

28    roasted brussels sprouts with brown butter & hazelnuts

30    garbanzo burgers with spicy mayo

31    pretty green lentils with bacon & feta

Reading "massaged" kale on restaurant menus always cracks me up. I have to admit, though, simply giving this superfood a bit of a rubdown works wonders—transforming its texture from coarse to silky. I like my kale with a lemony dressing and sticky-sweet dates and nuts, but kale Caesars are also having a moment. Or you could up the protein with hard-boiled egg, avocado, tomato, and sunflower seeds.

## massaged kale salad with dates & nuts

for the dressing

**1 clove garlic, mashed to a paste**

**Juice of 1 lemon**

**1 tablespoon honey**

**Salt and freshly ground pepper**

**$1/3$ cup (3 fl oz/80 ml) extra-virgin olive oil**

**1 bunch (about 8 large leaves) kale**

**1 cup (6 oz/185 g) Medjool dates**

**$1/4$ cup ($1 1/2$ oz/45 g) pine nuts**

**$1/4$ cup (1 oz/30 g) shaved Parmesan cheese**

*makes 4 servings*

To make the dressing, in a jar, combine the garlic, lemon juice, honey, ½ teaspoon salt, several grinds of pepper, and the olive oil. Shake to combine. Taste and adjust the seasoning, if necessary.

To prepare the kale, use a paring knife to remove and discard the stems. Tear the leaves into bite-size pieces. Place the kale in a large bowl. Massage for a few minutes, grabbing and squeezing handfuls of the leaves, just until they start to soften and feel silky.

To prepare the dates, use a paring knife to make a lengthwise slit, and remove and discard the long, narrow pits. Roughly chop the pitted dates. Add the dates and pine nuts to the bowl with the kale and toss to combine. Pour half of the dressing over the ingredients in the bowl, and toss to coat. Taste a leaf and add more dressing as needed, and save any remaining for another use.

Divide the salad between plates, sprinkle with the Parmesan, and serve.

*This is one of the most charming soups you'll ever meet: its thickness comes from the squash, its sweetness from the apple. Swirl in a spoonful of browned butter and drop a fragrant fried sage leaf on top, and the autumn flavors sing.*

# butternut squash soup with fried sage

4 tablespoons (2 oz/60 g) unsalted butter

1 yellow onion, chopped

1 large butternut squash (about 3 lb/1.5 kg), peeled, seeded, and cut into chunks

1 tart green apple, such as Granny Smith, peeled, cored, and cut into chunks

2 cups (16 fl oz/500 ml) chicken or vegetable stock

1 cup (8 fl oz/250 ml) dry hard cider or dry white wine

1 dried bay leaf

Salt and ground white pepper

1 bunch fresh sage

Slices extra-sharp Cheddar cheese for serving (optional)

*makes 6 servings*

In a Dutch oven over medium-high heat, melt 2 tablespoons of the butter. Add the onion and sauté until tender, about 5 minutes. Add the butternut squash and apple and cook for a few minutes longer. Add the stock, cider, and bay leaf. Bring to a boil, reduce the heat, and simmer until the squash is fork-tender and the liquid has slightly reduced, about 20–25 minutes.

Remove the soup from the heat and let cool slightly. Remove and discard the bay leaf. Working in batches if necessary, transfer the soup to a blender or use an immersion blender and puree until thick and smooth. Return to the Dutch oven and season with 1 teaspoon salt and ½ teaspoon white pepper. Taste and adjust the seasoning, if necessary. Keep warm over low heat.

Line a plate with paper towels. In a small sauté pan over medium heat, melt the remaining 2 tablespoons butter. Add two fresh sage leaves for each bowl you're planning on serving. Cook the sage leaves, turning once with tongs, until fragrant and just golden, a few minutes per side. Transfer to the paper towels.

Ladle the soup into bowls. Top each bowl with two fried sage leaves, and drizzle lightly with any remaining butter from the pan. Serve warm, passing the Cheddar at the table (see note, below), if you like.

Serving Tip: Fry only enough sage for the number of bowls you're serving, as the crispy edges won't keep. But the leaves are easy enough to make on their own, if you want leftovers later in the week. I like to slip a slice of crumbly, extra-sharp Cheddar down to the bottom of the bowl and scrape up melted bits with each bite.

... drop a fragrant fried sage leaf on top, and the autumn flavors sing.

Thick, creamy tomato soup is undeniably better when you make it yourself—and it's not hard. All you need are a handful of pantry staples and a blender. You could serve it with a crusty loaf of bread, or an old-school grilled cheese sandwich, but I'm partial to British-style toasties. Trick them out with caramelized onions, gooey cheese, and a dash of Worcestershire.

# creamy tomato soup & onion toasties

for the creamy tomato soup

1 tablespoon olive oil

1 yellow onion, chopped

$\frac{1}{2}$ teaspoon ground cloves

2 large cans (28 oz/875 g *each*) diced tomatoes, preferably San Marzano

2 cups (16 fl oz/500 ml) chicken or vegetable stock

1 dried bay leaf

$\frac{1}{2}$ cup (4 fl oz/125 ml) heavy cream (optional)

Salt and freshly ground pepper

for the onion toasties

2 tablespoons unsalted butter

1 yellow onion, halved lengthwise and thinly sliced

1 tablespoon firmly packed brown sugar

1 teaspoon Worcestershire sauce

4 thin slices country-style bread, halved

8 slices extra-sharp Cheddar cheese

makes 8 servings soup; 4 servings toasties

To make the creamy tomato soup, in a Dutch oven over medium-high heat, warm the olive oil. Add the onion and sauté until tender, about 5 minutes. Add the cloves and stir until fragrant, about 30 seconds. Add the tomatoes, stock, and bay leaf. Bring to a boil, reduce the heat, and simmer until the flavors have blended and the liquid has slightly reduced, about 20–25 minutes.

Remove the soup from the heat and let cool slightly. Remove and discard the bay leaf. Working in batches if necessary, transfer the soup to a blender or use an immersion blender and puree until thick but still slightly chunky. Return to the Dutch oven and add the cream, if using, and $\frac{1}{2}$ teaspoon salt and several grinds of pepper. Taste and adjust the seasoning, if necessary. Keep warm over low heat.

While the soup is simmering, make the onion toasties: In a sauté pan over medium heat, melt the butter. Add the onion and sauté until tender, about 5 minutes. Reduce the heat to low, sprinkle with the brown sugar and a pinch of salt, and continue to cook, stirring occasionally, until the onions have collapsed and caramelized, about 30 minutes. Drizzle with the Worcestershire sauce and stir to coat.

Preheat the oven to 350°F (180°C). Place the bread on a large rimmed baking sheet. Divide the caramelized onions between the slices of bread and top with the Cheddar. Bake until melted and bubbling, about 10 minutes.

Ladle the soup into bowls, place a couple of toasties on the side, and serve warm.

Leftovers Tip: Leftover tomato soup is seriously good stuff for lunches. This recipe yields twice as many servings of soup as toasties. But feel free to halve the recipe, if you like.

Hungarian mushroom soup is one of my family's favorites, featuring that magical trio of Eastern European flavors: sour cream, dill, and sweet paprika. I prefer to make it as a thick stew, textured with wild mushrooms and rich with beef broth. Spoon it over tender egg noodles drenched in butter. You won't be sorry.

# wild mushroom stew with dill & paprika

3 teaspoons olive oil,
or as needed

1 yellow onion, chopped

2 lb (1 kg) mixed mushrooms,
such as cremini, porcini, and
oyster, cut into bite-size pieces

1/4 cup (2 oz/60 g)
unsalted butter

1/4 cup (1 1/2 oz/45 g)
all-purpose flour

1/2 cup (4 fl oz/125 ml)
dry white wine

2 cups (16 fl oz/500 ml)
beef stock

1 tablespoon sweet paprika

1 tablespoon minced fresh dill,
or 1 1/2 teaspoons dried

Salt and freshly ground pepper

1/2 cup (4 oz/125 g) sour cream

Buttered egg noodles for serving

makes 4 to 6 servings

In a Dutch oven over medium-high heat, warm 1 teaspoon of the oil. Add the onion and sauté until tender, about 5 minutes. Transfer to a plate and set aside. Return the pan to the heat and add the remaining 2 teaspoons oil. Working in batches if necessary, add the mushrooms and sauté until they release their liquid, about 5 minutes. Transfer the mushrooms to the plate with the onion and set aside.

Return the pan to the stove, reduce the heat to medium, and melt the butter. Sprinkle with the flour, whisk to combine, and let bubble for 30 seconds. Slowly pour in the wine and stock and whisk frequently until thick, about 10 minutes. Stir in the reserved mushrooms and onion and the paprika, dill, 1/2 teaspoon salt, and several grinds of pepper. Taste and adjust the seasoning, if necessary. Simmer for a few minutes longer to let the flavors blend.

Remove from the heat and stir in the sour cream. Heap the buttered egg noodles onto plates, ladle the mushroom stew over, and serve warm.

Shopping Tip: Please note that 2 lb (1 kg) of mushrooms is actually a whole lot of mushrooms. Mushrooms lose liquid and shrink as they cook, so start big. In terms of varieties, I love wild for flavor, but I'm cheap, so I typically buy 1 lb (500 g) of something cultivated—like brown or button mushrooms, also known as cremini or baby bellas—and then augment with tree oysters, porcini, or whatever looks appealing.

Whether you're vegetarian, flexitarian, or just on a budget, everyone needs a great veggie chili to take some meat out of your week. I dump in three types of beans—black, red, and pink—and give them a kick with lots of cumin and chile. It's warm, filling, and comforting, and it's totally your call what you top it off with. This makes a big pot of beans, but chili only gets better the next day.

# three amigos bean chili

1 tablespoon olive oil

1 large yellow onion, chopped

3 cloves garlic, minced

1 fresh jalapeño chile, minced

2 teaspoons chile powder

1 teaspoon ground cumin

Salt

1 large can (28 oz/875 g) diced tomatoes, preferably San Marzano

1 cup (8 fl oz/250 ml) vegetable stock

1 dried bay leaf

1 can (15 oz/470 g) black beans, drained and rinsed

1 can (15 oz/470 g) pinto beans, drained and rinsed

1 can (15 oz/470 g) kidney beans, drained and rinsed

for serving

Sour cream

Shredded jack or Cheddar cheese, or crumbled queso fresco

Crushed tortilla chips

Chopped green onions

Sliced black olives, drained

makes 8 servings

In a Dutch oven over medium-high heat, warm the oil. Add the onion and sauté until tender, about 5 minutes. Add the garlic and fresh chile and stir until fragrant, about 2 minutes. Add the chile powder, cumin, and 1 teaspoon salt, and stir until fragrant, about 30 seconds.

Add the tomatoes, stock, and bay leaf. Bring to a boil, reduce the heat, and simmer until the liquid has slightly reduced, about 5 minutes. Add the black beans, pinto beans, and kidney beans and stir to combine. The chili should be very thick. Continue to simmer until the flavors have blended, about 20 minutes. Remove and discard the bay leaf. Taste and adjust the seasoning, if necessary.

Ladle the chili into bowls and serve warm, passing the toppings at the table.

Prep Tip: Fresh chiles carry most of their spiciness in the ribs and seeds. Remove the ribs and seeds from the jalapeño, if you prefer a little less heat.

*This is a great go-to dinner—super fresh and simple to throw together. Little baby shiitakes are delicious, but you can toss in whatever favorite veggies you have on hand. Carrots, sugar snap peas, or bell pepper strips add classic crunch. Fragrant sesame oil and seeds are the finishing touches.*

# asparagus & baby shiitake stir-fry

**for the stir-fry sauce**

**2 tablespoons soy sauce**

**2 tablespoons Mirin (see page 10)**

**1 tablespoon rice vinegar**

**1 tablespoon canola oil**

**2 cloves garlic, minced**

**1 tablespoon minced fresh ginger**

**3 green onions, white and pale green parts only, chopped**

**8 oz (250 g) baby shiitake mushrooms, halved or quartered**

**1 bunch asparagus, cut into bite-size pieces**

**1 can (8 oz/250 g) sliced water chestnuts, drained**

**Steamed brown rice for serving**

**Sesame oil for drizzling**

**Black sesame seeds for sprinkling**

*makes 4 servings*

To make the stir-fry sauce, in a small bowl, add the soy sauce, Mirin, and vinegar and whisk with a fork. Set aside.

In a large sauté pan or wok over medium-high heat, warm the oil. Add the garlic, ginger, and green onions and stir until fragrant, about 1 minute. Add the mushrooms and stir until they release their liquid, about 5 minutes. Add the asparagus, water chestnuts, and stir-fry sauce and stir just until the asparagus is bright green and tender-crisp and the sauce coats all of the ingredients, about 2 minutes.

Heap the rice onto plates and spoon the stir-fry on the side. Drizzle with sesame oil, sprinkle with sesame seeds, and serve warm.

Prep Tip: Stir-fry cooks in a flash, so make sure to do all of your mincing and chopping in advance, and have ingredients lined up and ready for action before you fire up the wok. Just think about what cooks slowest (carrots) versus fastest (peas), and order accordingly. Do you own a wok? Me neither. I use a sauté pan.

*This fast and fresh weeknight dinner delivers the comforts of pasta, red sauce, and cheese, but manages to stay light. I once read a food memoir where the author referred to eggplant as Italy's other meat, and I'm inclined to agree. In this case, a breadcrumb coating and a quick stint in a hot skillet develops a crisp crust.*

# eggplant parm

2 cups (16 fl oz/500 ml) Marinara (page 52), or your favorite jarred

Salt and freshly ground pepper

1 lb (500 g) dried linguine

Olive oil for drizzling and frying

2 large eggs

1 cup (2 oz/60 g) dried breadcrumbs

½ cup (2 oz/60 g) freshly grated Parmesan cheese, plus more for sprinkling

1 teaspoon dried basil

½ teaspoon dried oregano

1 large eggplant, thickly sliced lengthwise

*makes 4 servings*

In a saucepan over low heat, warm the marinara. Bring a large pot full of salted water to a boil. Add the linguine and cook until al dente, according to package directions. Drain and return to the pot. Drizzle with olive oil, toss, and cover to keep warm.

While the pasta is boiling, crack the eggs into a shallow bowl and whisk with a fork. Pour the breadcrumbs onto a plate and add the ½ cup Parmesan, basil, oregano, 1 teaspoon salt, and several grinds of pepper. Mix together with a fork or your fingers. Line up the eggplant, beaten eggs, and breadcrumb mixture on the counter. Place a clean plate at the end.

Working with one piece of eggplant at a time, dip it into the beaten eggs, letting any excess drip back into the bowl. Coat with the breadcrumbs, pressing gently to help them stick. Repeat with all of the eggplant, stacking the coated pieces on the plate at the end.

Preheat the oven to low (200°F/95°C). In a large nonstick frying pan over medium-high heat, warm several tablespoons of olive oil, enough to generously coat the bottom of the pan. Working in batches, fry the eggplant, turning once, until golden brown, about 5 minutes per side. Transfer the cooked eggplant slices to a baking dish or rimmed baking sheet, sprinkle with salt, and keep warm in the oven. Add more oil to the pan as needed between batches.

Divide the pasta between plates and place 2 or 3 slices of eggplant on the side. Ladle marinara over everything, sprinkle with additional Parmesan, grind with pepper, and serve warm.

Cooking Tip: Eggplant happily soaks up liquid, and will drink as much oil as you give it. To avoid using an unconscionable amount, start with a couple of tablespoons, keep an eye on your pan, and add a splash between batches as needed. You want just enough to coat the surface and maintain a mellow sizzle.

Some quesadillas I had at a Seattle farmers' market inspired this recipe. My friend Malavika took me to this hippie stand, where the aroma of dark greens, garlic, and cumin wafted off the griddle. We sat on the curb and tore into the cheesy triangles. Some bearded hipsters did a surprisingly good acoustic cover of Justin Timberlake's "My Love." True story.

## co-op quesadillas with beets & chard

1 bunch (about 8 large leaves) Swiss chard

1 tablespoon olive oil

$\frac{1}{2}$ yellow onion, sliced

1 large garnet beet, peeled, halved, and thinly sliced

1 fresh poblano chile, seeded and sliced

2 cloves garlic, minced

1 teaspoon ground cumin

1 teaspoon dried oregano

Salt and freshly ground pepper

4 large flour tortillas

2 cups (about 8 oz/250 g) shredded jack cheese

makes 4 servings

To prepare the chard, use a paring knife to remove the ribs. Chop the ribs and set aside. Tear the leaves into bite-size pieces and set aside.

In a large sauté pan over medium-high heat, warm the oil. Add the chard ribs, onion, beet, chile, and garlic. Sprinkle with the cumin, oregano, 1 teaspoon salt, and several grinds of pepper and stir to coat. Cook, stirring occasionally, until the garlic and cumin are fragrant and the vegetables are tender and starting to brown, about 5 minutes. Finally, add the chard leaves, and cook until the leaves are wilted, about 5 minutes. Taste and adjust the seasoning, if necessary. Remove from the heat.

Preheat the oven to low (200°F/95°C). In a large skillet over medium-high heat, place one of the tortillas. Sprinkle half of the tortilla with ¼ cup (1 oz/30 g) of the cheese, one fourth of the chard mixture, and top with another ¼ cup cheese. Fold the tortilla in half. Cook, turning once, until the tortilla is toasted and the cheese is melted, about 3 minutes per side. Transfer to a plate and keep warm in the oven. Repeat with the remaining tortillas, cheese, and veggies.

Slice the quesadillas into triangles, divide between plates, and serve warm.

Prep Tip: Think of Swiss chard as a vegetable with an identity crisis. The ribs cook at one rate, the leaves at another. You have to separate them to get it right. There are people in this world who throw away chard ribs, but they don't know what they're missing. They are so bittersweet, so tender, so good.

If we weren't dating, I'm pretty sure my grad-student boyfriend would live on microwave "baked" potatoes. The thing is, you can microwave potatoes in about 10 minutes. But they bake in just an hour, and require no additional effort. All you have to do is remember to plunk them on the oven rack. Planning ahead! It's what adults do! Rub the spuds with a dab of oil and a sprinkle of salt, for an extra crispy jacket. Load them up with any of your favorite fillings, from bacon and chives to saucy chicken curry.

# jacket potatoes with fillings

**4 large russet potatoes**

**Canola oil**

**Salt and freshly ground pepper**

**4 tablespoons (2 oz/60 g) unsalted butter**

for serving

**Shredded Cheddar cheese**

**Sour cream**

**Chopped chives or green onions**

**Crumbled cooked bacon**

**Sliced black olives, drained**

**Chopped steamed broccoli**

**Leftover taco meat (page 106)**

**Leftover chicken curry (page 86)**

**Leftover chili (page 21)**

*makes 4 servings*

Preheat the oven to 400°F (200°C). Rinse and dry the potatoes. Rub a dab of oil between your hands, and rub it all over the potatoes. Sprinkle generously with salt. Place the potatoes directly on the oven rack and bake until the skins are crispy and the centers are soft when pierced with a fork, about 60–70 minutes, depending on the size of your potatoes.

When the potatoes are cool enough to handle, split them lengthwise. Fluff the centers with a fork. Divide the butter between the steaming potato halves, letting it melt into the flesh.

Place the potatoes on plates, load with your favorite toppings, and serve warm.

*I have a theory that anyone who objects to brussels sprouts has never had them cooked properly. Please don't steam, boil, or otherwise abuse them. Roasting brings out their best, revealing a beautiful little cabbage: nutty, peppery, crinkled leaves on the outside, tender at heart. Hazelnuts play to brussels sprouts' natural nuttiness, and the vinegar from a handful of capers cuts through the richness of brown butter and sheep's milk cheese.*

# roasted brussels sprouts with brown butter & hazelnuts

1½ lb (750 g) brussels sprouts, trimmed and halved

3 tablespoons olive oil

3 cloves garlic, minced

Salt and freshly ground pepper

2 tablespoons unsalted butter

¼ cup (2 oz/60 g) capers

½ cup (2½ oz/75 g) hazelnuts, coarsely chopped

1 tablespoon fresh thyme leaves

⅓ cup (1½ oz/45 g) freshly grated pecorino cheese

*makes 4 to 6 servings*

Preheat the oven to 450°F (230°C). In a large bowl, add the brussels sprouts, drizzle with the olive oil, and toss to coat. Add the garlic, ½ teaspoon salt, and a generous grind of pepper and toss again. Spread on a large rimmed baking sheet. Roast, stirring once during cooking, until the leaves start to crinkle and turn crispy, about 15 minutes.

While the brussels sprouts are roasting, in a small frying pan over medium-high heat, melt the butter. Add the capers and hazelnuts. Cook, shaking the pan occasionally, until a few of the capers have burst and the nuts turn fragrant and golden, about 5 minutes. Watch to make sure the butter doesn't burn.

Transfer the brussels sprouts to a large bowl, drizzle with the butter, capers, and nuts, add the thyme, and toss to combine. Sprinkle with the pecorino and grind with pepper. Taste and adjust the seasoning, if necessary (the capers and pecorino may add enough salt already). Serve warm.

### Veggie Hacks: Bacon & Shallots

Instead of capers, nuts, and cheese, you can toss roasted brussels sprouts with other salty seasonings. In a small frying pan over medium-high heat, fry **4 thick slices bacon, chopped**. Transfer to a plate. Drain off all but about 1 tablespoon of the bacon grease. Add **2 large shallots, thinly sliced and separated into rings**. Sauté for about 5 minutes, until golden. Add the bacon and shallots to the large bowl with the roasted brussels sprouts, toss to combine, grind generously with pepper, and serve warm.

We've all had regrettable veggie burgers from the freezer aisle. They bear a strong resemblance to hockey pucks. You deserve better. The from-scratch version is super tender, bound with mashed beans, studded with carrots and corn, and topped with fresh veggies and a swipe of spicy mayo. I recommend garbanzos, but feel free to use black beans, or any other variety that you like. Wrap leftover patties and stow them in the fridge or freezer—look, you just created your own convenience food.

# garbanzo burgers with spicy mayo

for the spicy mayo

½ cup (4 fl oz/125 ml) mayo

1 tablespoon harissa (see note)

Salt

1 can (15 oz/470 g) garbanzo beans, drained and rinsed

2 large eggs

½ small yellow onion, finely chopped

1 carrot, finely chopped

½ cup (3 oz/90 g) corn kernels, thawed if frozen

1 clove garlic, minced

¼ cup (⅓ oz/10 g) fresh cilantro leaves, finely chopped

⅓ cup (1½ oz/45 g) dried breadcrumbs

1 tablespoon olive oil

for serving

Whole-wheat burger buns

Sliced tomato

Sliced avocado

Sprouts

makes 4 servings

To make the spicy mayo, in a small bowl, add the mayo, harissa, and a pinch of salt and whisk with a fork. Cover and refrigerate until ready to serve.

In a food processor, combine the garbanzo beans and eggs, and blend until thick and chunky. (If you don't have a food processor, you can mash by hand.) Transfer to a large bowl and stir in the onion, carrot, corn, garlic, cilantro, and 1 teaspoon salt. Fold in the breadcrumbs, just until combined. You should have a thick batter.

In a large frying pan over medium-high heat, warm the oil. Dollop the batter into the pan, pressing and smoothing gently to form 4 patties. Cook, turning once, until golden brown, about 5 minutes per side.

Place the burger buns on plates, top with the patties, and drizzle with the spicy mayo. Serve, passing the tomato, avocado, and sprouts at the table.

Shopping Tip: Harissa is a fiery North African condiment, made from a blend of red peppers. Look for it with the other international ingredients at your grocery store. Just a spoonful transforms humble mayo into a flavorful spread.

*A word on lentils: They're not just for vegetarians. In fact, they're even better with bacon! Embrace the French tradition, and toss them with lardons (fancy bacon), feta, and a mustardy vinaigrette. Serve with dry white wine, a baguette and sweet butter, and a tangle of frisee.*

# pretty green lentils with bacon & feta

1 cup (7 oz/220 g) dried
French green lentils

Salt and freshly ground pepper

4 oz (125 g) lardons or
diced pancetta

1 large shallot, finely chopped

1 tablespoon Dijon mustard

1 tablespoon red wine vinegar

1/4 cup (2 fl oz/60 ml) olive oil

1 tablespoon fresh thyme leaves

1 cup (5 oz/155 g) crumbled
feta cheese

*makes 4 servings*

In a pot, add the lentils, 2½ cups (20 fl oz/625 ml) cold water, and a pinch of salt. Bring to a boil, reduce the heat, and simmer until tender, according to package directions. Drain and return to the pot.

While the lentils are cooking, in a sauté pan over medium-high heat, fry the lardons until crispy, about 3 minutes. Add the shallot and stir just to take the raw edge off, 1 minute. Scrape into the pot with the lentils.

In a small bowl, add the mustard, vinegar, olive oil, and several grinds of pepper and whisk with a fork. Pour over the lentils and lardons, and toss to coat. Fold in the thyme and feta last. Taste and adjust the seasoning, if necessary (the lardons and feta may add enough salt already).

Spoon the lentils onto plates, grind with pepper, and serve.

Shopping Tip: Make sure you grab the right kind of lentils at the grocery store. French lentils from the le Puy region look like dark green little pebbles, and unlike some of their international cousins, they hold their shape when cooked. Yellow, red, and brown lentils tend to collapse, so they're better suited for dal, soups, and stews.

# chapter 2: cheap carbs
## pasta, pizza & grains

35    quinoa with roasted summer vegetables

36    farro with roasted winter vegetables

39    spring vegetable risotto

40    wild mushroom risotto

41    gingery pork lo mein with shiitakes & bok choy

42    sriracha fried rice with sunny eggs

45    tossed pasta remixes

46    mac & cheese with garlicky breadcrumbs

48    meaty lasagne

49    panfried gnocchi with chicken, lemon & thyme

51    tortellini en brodo with kale

52    pizza basics

55    pizza remixes

Quinoa (keen-wah) has reached crazy trendy superfood status, largely because it's a grain that's a complete protein. It feels redundant to me to plate it next to chicken or fish. But then I started working quinoa into fresh, fast veggie dinners, and I fell hard. Try a summer medley of meaty eggplant, tender squash and zucchini, vibrant bell pepper, and a burst of cherry tomatoes. Grilling the veggies adds terrific smoky flavor, but on busy weeknights, just pop a baking sheet into the oven.

# quinoa with roasted summer vegetables

1 small zucchini, diced

1 small summer squash, diced

1 small Japanese eggplant, diced

1 bell pepper, seeded and diced

Olive oil for drizzling

Salt and freshly ground pepper

1 cup (7 oz/220 g) quinoa

1 cup (6 oz/185 g) cherry tomatoes, halved lengthwise

8 oz (250 g) fresh mozzarella cheese, drained and torn into bite-size pieces

1/4 cup (2 fl oz/60 ml) premade fresh basil pesto

*makes 4 to 6 servings*

Preheat the oven to 400°F (200°C). On a large rimmed baking sheet, add the zucchini, summer squash, eggplant, and bell pepper. Drizzle with olive oil and toss to coat. Season generously with salt and pepper. Roast until tender and starting to brown, about 20 minutes.

While the vegetables are roasting, in a pot over medium-high heat, toast the dry quinoa until fragrant, about 1 minute. Add water and cook until tender, according to package directions. Fluff with a fork and set aside.

In a large bowl, add the cherry tomatoes and fresh mozzarella. Drizzle the pesto over and toss to coat. Add the roasted vegetables and cooked quinoa and toss to combine. Taste and adjust the seasoning, if necessary.

Spoon the quinoa and vegetables into bowls, grind with pepper, and serve.

Leftovers Tip: Leftover grains are great fodder for lunches. Quinoa or farro with veggies (page 36) hold up beautifully, even at room temperature for a few hours.

Farro is an ancient grain that gets great press. It's a pleasantly chewy variety of wheat that's been noshed on by Italian peasants for hundreds of years. Today, health nuts are all over it, thanks to its high fiber and rich vitamins. Cook yourself a pot, and fold in sweet root veggies, crumbled cheese, and fragrant thyme for a virtuous but deliciously textured salad.

# farro with roasted winter vegetables

**Salt and freshly ground pepper**

**1 cup (7 oz/220 g) semi-pearled farro (see note)**

**1 large carrot, peeled and diced**

**1 large parsnip, peeled and diced**

**2 garnet beets, peeled and diced**

**Olive oil for drizzling**

**2 tablespoons red wine vinegar**

**2 tablespoons chopped fresh thyme leaves**

**1 cup (5 oz/155 g) crumbled feta cheese**

**Sunflower seeds for sprinkling**

*makes 6 servings*

Bring a pot full of salted water to a boil. Add the farro and cook until tender, according to package directions. Drain and return to the pot.

While the farro is cooking, preheat the oven to 400°F (200°C). On a large rimmed baking sheet, add the carrot, parsnip, and beets. Drizzle with olive oil and toss to coat. Season generously with salt and pepper. Roast until tender and crispy at the edges, about 30 minutes.

Drizzle the farro with the vinegar and toss to coat. Add the roasted vegetables and toss to combine. Fold in the thyme and feta last. Taste and adjust the seasoning, if necessary.

Spoon the farro and vegetables into bowls, sprinkle with sunflower seeds, grind with pepper, and serve.

Shopping Tip: Look for semi-pearled farro, which is low maintenance. The whole-grain variety requires soaking, and a little more planning ahead.

But risotto is hard, you say. Not true! Risotto is a 30-minute meal made in one pot with ingredients you probably already have in the pantry. The hardest part is stirring for 20-odd minutes. I call my mom when I make risotto. It's a nice set window, so if she really gets going, it's, "Sorry, Mom, dinner's ready!" This spring medley stars bright green veggies with a zip of lemon. Snap up English peas at the farmers' market and use them the same day, shelling just before cooking. If that's too much fuss, frozen will do fine.

# spring vegetable risotto

2 tablespoons olive oil

2 cloves garlic, minced

1½ cups (10½ oz/330 g) Arborio rice

1 cup (8 fl oz/250 ml) dry white wine

4½ cups (36 fl oz/1.1 l) chicken stock

½ bunch asparagus, cut into bite-size pieces

½ cup (2 oz/60 g) sugar snap peas

½ cup (2½ oz/75 g) English peas, fresh or frozen

½ cup (2 oz/60 g) freshly grated Parmesan cheese, plus more for sprinkling

Grated zest and juice of 1 lemon

Salt and freshly ground pepper

*makes 4 servings*

In a Dutch oven over medium heat, warm the olive oil. Add the garlic and stir until fragrant, about 1 minute. Add the rice, stir to coat, and toast for a few minutes, taking care not to let the garlic brown.

Set the timer for 25 minutes. Reduce the heat to medium-low and slowly start adding liquid, one ladleful at a time: first the wine and then the stock. Stir frequently until the liquid is soaked up and the rice starts to stick to the bottom of the pan. How much liquid you'll need depends on how fast you simmer and how frequently you add, so pace yourself, stirring in about ½ cup (4 fl oz/125 ml) every few minutes.

In the last few minutes of cooking, when the rice is nearly tender, add the asparagus, sugar snaps, and peas. Cook just until the vegetables are bright green and tender-crisp. Remove from the heat and fold in the ½ cup Parmesan and lemon zest and juice. Taste and adjust the seasoning, if necessary (the stock and Parmesan may add enough salt already).

Ladle the risotto and vegetables into bowls, sprinkle with Parmesan, grind with pepper, and serve warm.

Risotto Hacks: Arincini

Have you ever had arincini? They're what happen when risotto dies and goes to heaven. If you have some **plain risotto** without the mushrooms or spring veggies chilling in the fridge, you can shape it into balls, poke **small cubes of mozzarella** inside, and fry them in **olive oil** until crisp and brown. A **pinch of saffron** in the chicken stock that you use to make the risotto takes it to the maestro level.

*This creamy, comforting risotto uses both fresh and dried mushrooms to reach the fullest flavor. Dried mushrooms add extra depth, infusing everything with their potent, earthy nature. Make sure to save the liquid from soaking the mushrooms, and add it to the pan. A spoonful of truffle oil and a handful of rosemary leaves bring together the woodsy aroma.*

# wild mushroom risotto

1 oz (30 g) dried porcini mushrooms

1½ cups (12 fl oz/375 ml) boiled water

2 tablespoons olive oil

8 oz (250 g) mixed fresh mushrooms, such as cremini, porcini, and oyster, cut into bite-size pieces

2 cloves garlic, minced

1 shallot, minced

1½ cups (10½ oz/330 g) Arborio rice

1 cup (8 fl oz/250 ml) dry white wine

2 cups (16 fl oz/500 ml) beef stock

½ cup (2 oz/60 g) freshly grated Parmesan cheese, plus more for sprinkling

1 tablespoon minced fresh rosemary leaves

1 teaspoon black truffle oil

Salt and freshly ground pepper

*makes 4 servings*

In a small bowl, soak the dried mushrooms in the hot water for 30 minutes. Scoop out the mushrooms, transfer to a cutting board, and roughly chop. Strain the soaking liquid into a clean bowl and set aside.

In a Dutch oven over medium-high heat, warm 1 tablespoon of the olive oil. Add the fresh mushrooms and sauté until they release their liquid, about 5 minutes. Transfer to a plate and set aside.

Return the pan to medium heat and add the remaining 1 tablespoon olive oil, the garlic, and the shallot and stir until fragrant, about 1 minute. Add the rice, stir to coat, and toast for a few minutes, taking care not to let the garlic brown.

Set the timer for 25 minutes. Reduce the heat to medium-low and slowly start adding liquid, one ladleful at a time: first the wine, then the reserved mushroom broth, finishing with the stock. Stir frequently until the liquid is soaked up and the rice starts to stick to the bottom of the pan. How much liquid you'll need depends on how fast you simmer and how frequently you add, so pace yourself, stirring in about ½ cup (4 fl oz/125 ml) every few minutes.

In the last few minutes of cooking, when the rice is nearly tender, add all of the reserved mushrooms. Stir until warmed through. Remove from the heat and fold in the ½ cup Parmesan, rosemary, and truffle oil. Taste and adjust the seasoning, if necessary (the stock and Parmesan may add enough salt already).

Ladle the risotto and mushrooms into bowls, sprinkle with Parmesan, grind with pepper, and serve warm.

Shopping Tip: When cooking with wine, I'd recommend sticking to dry whites and reds, and not going any lower than $10 to $15 a bottle. It's your budget and your call, but it would be a shame to douse lovely mushrooms—not to mention your efforts—in substandard vino.

*Tired of greasy takeout? Want to save some money? Toss fresh egg noodles with thin strips of tender pork, meaty shiitake mushrooms, and refreshing little cabbage leaves. If you crave Asian flavors, stock up on the staples (see page 10). The bottles all keep well in the fridge, and you'll enjoy them again and again in flavorful stir-fries, noodles, soups, and veggies.*

# gingery pork lo mein with shiitakes & bok choy

for the stir-fry sauce

¹/₄ cup (2 fl oz/60 ml) oyster sauce (see page 10)

¹/₄ cup (2 fl oz/60 ml) soy sauce

2 tablespoons Mirin (see page 10)

1 boneless pork chop (about ¹/₂ lb/250 g)

10 oz (315 g) dried Chinese egg noodles

1 tablespoon sesame oil, plus more for drizzling

2 cloves garlic, minced

1 tablespoon minced fresh ginger

3 green onions, white and pale green parts only, chopped

8 oz (250 g) baby shiitake mushrooms, halved or quartered

1 small bok choy, cut into wide strips

Black sesame seeds for sprinkling

*makes 4 servings*

To make the stir-fry sauce, in a small bowl, add the oyster sauce, soy sauce, and Mirin and whisk with a fork. Place the pork chop inside a zippered plastic bag, pour half of the stir-fry sauce over, and seal. Massage the bag to coat the pork chop with the sauce. Refrigerate and marinate for 30 minutes. Set aside the remaining sauce.

While the pork is marinating, bring a pot full of salted water to a boil. Add the noodles and cook until al dente, according to package directions. Drain, rinse under cold running water, and return to the pot. Drizzle with sesame oil and toss.

In a large sauté pan or wok over medium-high heat, warm 1 tablespoon sesame oil. Add the pork chop and sear until browned, about 3 minutes per side. Reduce the heat to medium-low and continue to cook until the pork is nearly firm but still pale pink and juicy at the center, about 10 minutes. Transfer to a cutting board and let rest briefly. Slice into strips.

Return the pan to medium-high heat and add the garlic, ginger, and green onions and stir until fragrant, about 1 minute. Add the mushrooms and stir until they release their liquid, 5 minutes. Add the bok choy and stir just until the leaves have wilted, 2 minutes. Add the pork, noodles, and remaining stir-fry sauce and cook until warmed through and the sauce coats all of the ingredients, about 2 minutes.

Divide the lo mein between bowls, sprinkle with sesame seeds, and serve warm.

*If you've got leftover rice lurking in the back of the fridge, veggies kicking it in the freezer, and a bottle of Sriracha in your cupboard, you've got what it takes to make killer fried rice. I slide a sunnyside-up fried egg on top, because eggs are cheap, and buttery yolks make my heart skip a beat. But you could fold in some chicken, prawns, or Chinese sausage, if you like.*

# sriracha fried rice with sunny eggs

for the stir-fry sauce

¼ cup (2 fl oz/60 ml) soy sauce

2 tablespoons Mirin
(see page 10)

2 tablespoons Sriracha sauce
(see page 10), plus more for
drizzling

4 tablespoons (2 fl oz/60 ml)
canola oil

2 cloves garlic, minced

1 tablespoon minced fresh ginger

2 green onions, white and pale
green parts only, chopped

1 large carrot, chopped

4 cups (1¼ lb/625 g) cold
cooked rice

1 cup (5 oz/155 g) fresh or
frozen peas

1 cup (5 oz/155 g) fresh or
frozen edamame

4 large eggs

*makes 4 servings*

To make the stir-fry sauce, in a small bowl, add the soy sauce, Mirin, and Sriracha and whisk with a fork. Set aside.

Preheat the oven to low (200°F/95°C). In a large nonstick frying pan over medium-high heat, warm 2 tablespoons of the oil. Add the garlic, ginger, and green onions and stir until fragrant, about 1 minute. Add the carrot and stir until it starts to soften, about 2 minutes. Add the rice and let sizzle, about 5 minutes. Add the peas, edamame, and stir-fry sauce and stir just until the peas are bright green and heated through and the sauce coats all of the ingredients, about 2 minutes. Divide the fried rice between four oven-safe bowls and pop into the oven to keep warm.

Wipe out the frying pan. Return the pan to medium heat and warm the remaining 2 tablespoons oil. Crack the eggs into the pan and cook until the whites are set but the yolks are still runny, about 3 minutes.

Slide a fried egg on top of each bowl of fried rice, drizzle with additional Sriracha, and serve warm.

Pasta is a quick, cheap dinner, but it's easy to get into a grocery rut: box of spaghetti, jar of marinara, blah. Keep it fresh with four different flavor profiles, all equally easy to toss together.

# tossed pasta remixes

*each recipe makes 4 servings*

## twists with tomatoes, olives & fresh mozzarella

½ lb (250 g) dried rotini or your favorite twisted pasta

Olive oil for drizzling

2 cups (12 oz/375 g) halved cherry tomatoes

½ cup (2 oz/60 g) briny black olives, such as Kalamata

4 oz (125 g) fresh mozzarella cheese, drained and torn

Salt and freshly ground pepper

Handful of fresh basil leaves, torn

Cook the pasta according to package directions. Drain and return to the pot. Drizzle with olive oil and toss to coat. Add the tomatoes, olives, and mozzarella and toss to combine. Season with salt and pepper. Fold in the basil and serve warm.

## shells with grilled shrimp, arugula & feta

Juice of ½ lemon

2 tablespoons olive oil

4 cloves garlic, minced

¼ teaspoon red pepper flakes

Salt and freshly ground pepper

1 lb (500 g) raw shrimp, peeled but tail on

½ lb (250 g) dried conchiglie or your favorite round pasta

½ cup (4 fl oz/125 ml) premade fresh arugula pesto

½ cup (2½ oz/75 g) crumbled feta, plus more for sprinkling

In a large bowl, add the lemon juice, olive oil, garlic, red pepper flakes, ½ teaspoon salt, and a generous grind of pepper and whisk with a fork. Add the shrimp and turn to coat. Marinate, turning occasionally, about 15 minutes. Preheat a grill or grill pan to medium-high heat. Cook the shrimp until bright pink and curled, 2 minutes per side. Cook the pasta according to package directions. Drain and return to the pot. Add the pesto, the grilled shrimp, and feta and toss to combine. Sprinkle with feta, grind with pepper, and serve warm.

## tubes with chicken, zucchini, peppers & pesto

2 tablespoons olive oil

1 small zucchini, sliced

1 red bell pepper, seeded and cut into bite-size pieces

2 cups (12 oz/375 g) cooked shredded chicken

½ lb (250 g) dried penne or your favorite tube pasta

½ cup (4 fl oz/125 ml) premade fresh basil pesto

Freshly grated Parmesan for sprinkling

Freshly ground pepper

In a large sauté pan over medium-high heat, warm the oil. Add the zucchini and pepper and cook just until tender, about 3 minutes. Add the chicken and stir to warm through, 2 minutes. Cook the pasta according to package directions. Drain and return to the pot. Add the pesto and the chicken, zucchini, and pepper and toss to combine. Sprinkle with Parmesan, grind with pepper, and serve warm.

## ties with spinach, mushrooms & artichoke

2 tablespoons olive oil

8 oz (250 g) sliced mushrooms

2 cloves garlic, minced

8 oz (250 g) fresh spinach leaves

Salt and freshly ground pepper

½ lb (250 g) dried farfalle or your favorite bow-tie pasta

½ cup (4 fl oz/125 ml) premade fresh Alfredo sauce

½ cup (2 oz/60 g) marinated artichoke hearts, roughly chopped

Freshly grated Parmesan for sprinkling

In a large sauté pan over medium-high heat, warm the oil. Add the mushrooms and sauté until they release their liquid, about 5 minutes. Add the garlic and stir until fragrant, 1 minute. Add the spinach and stir until wilted, 1 minute. Season with salt and pepper. Cook the pasta according to package directions. Drain and return to the pot. Add the Alfredo sauce, the cooked mushrooms and spinach, and the artichoke hearts and toss to combine. Sprinkle with Parmesan, grind with pepper, and serve warm.

*If I invite friends over last minute, I make homemade mac topped with a crisp crust of breadcrumbs. Start with butter and flour, the building blocks of white sauce, and then craft the gooey goodness your way. Sharp, flavorful cheeses like Cheddar, Gruyère, or Parmesan lend the most character.*

# mac & cheese with garlicky breadcrumbs

Salt and freshly ground pepper

1 lb (500 g) dried elbow macaroni, or your favorite small shape of pasta

Olive oil for drizzling

2 tablespoons unsalted butter

3 tablespoons all-purpose flour

Pinch of ground nutmeg

1 teaspoon dry mustard

2 cups (16 fl oz/500 ml) milk, warmed

3 cups (12 oz/375 g) shredded sharp Cheddar cheese

for the breadcrumbs

2 tablespoons unsalted butter

2 cloves garlic, minced

1 cup (4 oz/125 g) dried breadcrumbs

*makes 8 servings*

Preheat the oven to 350°F (180°C). Butter a large casserole pan.

Bring a large pot full of salted water to a boil. Add the pasta and cook according to package directions, stopping 1 minute before the shortest suggested time. Drain, rinse with cold water, and return to the pot. Drizzle with olive oil, toss, and set aside.

While the macaroni is cooking, in a saucepan over medium heat, melt the 2 tablespoons butter. Add the flour, nutmeg, and mustard, whisk to combine, and let bubble for 30 seconds. Slowly pour in the milk and whisk frequently until thick, about 10 minutes. Remove from the heat and add the Cheddar and 1½ teaspoons salt, stirring until the cheese melts. Pour the cheese sauce over the pasta and stir to coat. Scrape the macaroni and cheese into the prepared pan.

To make the breadcrumbs, in a large frying pan over medium heat, melt the 2 tablespoons butter. Add the garlic and stir until fragrant, about 1 minute. Add the breadcrumbs and stir until they are coated and start to smell toasted, about 5 minutes. Sprinkle over the macaroni and cheese.

Bake until golden brown, about 30–35 minutes. Spoon the macaroni and cheese into bowls, grind with pepper, and serve warm.

## Mac Hacks

Lobster Mac: Poach **1½ lb (750 g) lobster in the shell**, approximately 4 tails and 4 claws (see page 72). Shell and chop the meat and stir into the macaroni before topping with the breadcrumbs. Sprinkle with **chopped chives** before serving.

Chard Mac: Sauté **1 bunch (about 8 large leaves) Swiss chard**, ribs and leaves separated and chopped, with **2 cloves minced garlic** (see page 110). Stir into the macaroni and cheese before topping with the breadcrumbs.

Truffled Mac: Sauté **1 lb (500 g) mixed mushrooms**, such as cremini, porcini, and oyster, cut into bite-size pieces, with **2 cloves minced garlic**. Add a **handful of fresh thyme leaves** and stir into the macaroni before topping with the breadcrumbs. Drizzle lightly with **truffle oil** before serving.

Bacon Mac: Stir **8 thick slices cooked, crumbled bacon** into the macaroni and cheese before topping with the breadcrumbs. Grind generously with coarse black pepper before serving.

My boyfriend once said, "Lasagne is the worst. You cook it and then you still have to cook it." I won't lie to you. There is some assembly involved. But it's not hard, it's a fun Sunday project, and you get to feast on leftover lasagne all week. This version features a rich Bolognese, but for even bigger flavor, you could swap in some spicy Italian sausage for part of the ground beef.

# meaty lasagne

for the spinach filling

2 tablespoons olive oil

1 yellow onion, finely chopped

5 cloves garlic, minced

1 lb (500 g) baby spinach

1 cup (8 oz/250 g) fresh ricotta cheese, whole or part skim

1 large egg, lightly beaten

1/2 teaspoon *each* dried oregano, basil, and thyme

Salt and freshly ground pepper

for the beef filling

1 lb (500 g) lean ground beef

1/2 cup (4 fl oz/125 ml) dry red wine

2 cups (16 fl oz/500 ml) Marinara (page 52), or your favorite jarred

for the white sauce

2 tablespoons unsalted butter

2 tablespoons all-purpose flour

Pinch of ground nutmeg

2 cups (16 fl oz/500 ml) milk, warmed

1/2 cup (2 oz/60 g) freshly grated Parmesan cheese

1 lb (500 g) dried lasagne (about 16 sheets)

1 cup (4 oz/125 g) shredded mozzarella cheese

*makes 8 to 10 servings*

To make the spinach filling, in a large sauté pan over medium-high heat, warm the olive oil. Add the onion and sauté until tender, about 5 minutes. Add the garlic and stir until fragrant, 1 minute. Transfer half of the mixture to a plate and set aside. Return the pan to the heat and add the spinach, working in batches if necessary, covering with the lid and stirring occasionally until wilted. (It's a big pile at first, but it cooks way down.) Transfer to a large bowl and let cool. Add the ricotta, egg, oregano, basil, thyme, 1 teaspoon salt, and a grind of pepper. Stir and set aside.

To make the beef filling, wipe out the pan and return to medium-high heat. Add the reserved onions and garlic and the beef, breaking it up with a spatula. Sprinkle with 1 teaspoon of salt and a grind of pepper. Let the beef cook for a few minutes undisturbed, until it starts to develop a sear. Stir and break up any larger pieces. Cook until the beef is browned, a few minutes longer. Reduce the heat to low and add the wine, scraping up any browned bits on the bottom of the pan. Add the marinara, adjust the heat, and simmer until the flavors have blended, 10 minutes.

To make the white sauce, in a saucepan over medium heat, melt the butter. Sprinkle with the flour and nutmeg, whisk to combine, and let bubble for 30 seconds. Slowly pour in the milk and whisk frequently until thick, about 10 minutes. Remove from the heat and add the Parmesan and a pinch of salt and stir to combine.

Preheat the oven to 350°F (180°C). Set out a 9-by-13-inch (23-by-33-cm) baking pan, and line up all of the ingredients on the counter: white sauce, beef filling, and spinach filling. Pour half of the white sauce into the bottom of the pan, tilting and spreading evenly with a spatula. Lay down sheets of pasta, overlapping slightly if necessary. Pour in the beef filling, spreading evenly. Add another layer of pasta. Pour in the spinach filling. Add a final layer of pasta. Pour the remaining white sauce over. Sprinkle with the mozzarella. Cover the pan tightly with foil (see note).

Bake until the pasta is tender, about 30 minutes, then remove the foil and bake until the cheese is golden and bubbling, about 10 minutes longer. Let rest for a few minutes. Cut the lasagne into squares, transfer to plates, and serve warm.

Prep Tip: Some recipes insist on parboiling the noodles first, but I keep it easy. You can sneak by, as long as you make sure the pasta is submerged in sauce, and you wrap the pan tightly with foil. Uncover briefly for that bubbling golden topping.

Gnocchi can be found among the packs of fresh pasta in the deli case. They're cheap and filling, and easy to toss with marinara (page 52), basil pesto, or any sauce you like. But I love them simply seared in a hot pan with a drizzle of olive oil and a shower of Parmesan and lemon zest. Fold in chicken to make it a full meal. Think chicken and dumplings—gnocchi are, after all, little potato dumplings—only faster.

# panfried gnocchi with chicken, lemon & thyme

2 tablespoons olive oil

12 oz (375 g) fresh gnocchi

2 cups (12 oz/375 g) cooked shredded chicken

Salt and freshly ground pepper

2 tablespoons unsalted butter

1/4 cup (2 fl oz/60 ml) heavy cream

Grated zest of 1 lemon, and juice of 1/2 lemon

1/4 cup (1 oz/30 g) freshly grated Parmesan cheese, plus more for sprinkling

Handful fresh thyme leaves, chopped

makes 4 servings

In a large nonstick frying pan over medium-high heat, warm the olive oil. Add the gnocchi and sauté until golden brown and crisp, about 5 minutes. Add the chicken and stir until warmed through. Season with 1/2 teaspoon salt and a generous grind of pepper. Transfer to a large bowl and keep warm.

Return the pan to the heat and melt the butter. Add the cream, lemon juice, and Parmesan and stir until the cheese has melted (it will still be a little grainy). Pour the sauce over the gnocchi and turn to coat. Fold in the lemon zest and thyme last. Taste and adjust the seasoning, if necessary.

Spoon the gnocchi into bowls, sprinkle with Parmesan, grind with pepper, and serve warm.

Just 10 minutes start to finish and you have tortellini en brodo, a comforting Italian soup. All you have to do is bring a rich beef broth to a gentle simmer, add stuffed pasta and a handful of dark greens, and wait until they get plump and tender. Use the best fresh tortellini you can find, filled with fluffy ricotta or savory sausage. If you have a good mom-and-pop deli in your neighborhood, you're in luck.

# tortellini en brodo with kale

½ bunch (about 4 large leaves) kale

6 cups (48 fl oz/1.5 l) beef stock

1 clove garlic, smashed but left whole

1 Parmesan rind (optional)

12 oz (375 g) cheese or meat tortellini

Freshly grated Parmesan cheese for sprinkling

Freshly ground pepper

makes 4 servings

To prepare the kale, use a paring knife to remove and discard the stems. Tear the leaves into bite-size pieces.

In a pot over medium-high heat, bring the stock to a simmer. Add the garlic and Parmesan rind, if using, reduce the heat, and simmer for 10 minutes to let the flavors blend.

Add the tortellini and kale leaves and cook until the tortellini are tender, according to package directions, and the kale turns bright green. Discard the garlic clove and Parmesan rind.

Ladle tortellini and broth into bowls, sprinkle with grated Parmesan, grind with pepper, and serve warm.

Housekeeping Tip: Save old Parmesan rinds! Even when you've grated them most of the way down. They'll last for weeks at the back of the cheese drawer, and they add salty complexity when slipped into stocks or soups.

It was a major post-grad revelation when I realized that, as much as I had relied on takeout pizza, I actually prefer the DIY version. Sure, I knew homemade pizza would be healthier, without the extra oil and salt that restaurants add. What I didn't appreciate was how much tastier it is. Now, thanks to the fresh balls of dough found at many grocery stores, homemade is also Friday-night easy.

# pizza basics

## basic technique: prepping pizza dough

**1 ball (about 1 lb/500 g) fresh pizza dough**

**Corn or all-purpose flour for dusting**

**Olive oil for brushing**

**Salt and freshly ground pepper**

*makes 1 pizza*

About 30 minutes before you're ready to start cooking, take the pizza dough out of the refrigerator and let it come to room temperature on the counter. Preheat the oven to 500°F (260°C). Turn the dough out onto a large work surface dusted with flour. Roll it out into a thin round. Let it rest for 10 minutes, then roll it out a second time. Dust a baking sheet with flour, and transfer the dough to the prepared sheet. Brush the dough with olive oil and sprinkle with salt.

Prep Tip: The best trick I've learned for rolling out pizza dough is to start at room temperature and roll it out twice. Let the dough rest for a good 10 minutes between—no poking, no prodding!—to allow the glutens to relax and stop fighting back.

## basic recipe: marinara

**1 tablespoon olive oil**

**1 small onion, minced**

**2 or 3 cloves garlic, minced**

**1 large can (28 oz/875 g) diced tomatoes, preferably San Marzano**

**1 cup (8 fl oz/250 ml) dry red wine**

**$1/8$ teaspoon red pepper flakes**

**1 teaspoon *each* dried oregano, basil, and thyme**

**Salt and freshly ground pepper**

*makes about 4 cups (32 fl oz/1 l)*

In a Dutch oven over medium-high heat, warm the oil. Add the onion and sauté until tender, about 5 minutes. Add the garlic and stir until fragrant, about 2 minutes. Add the tomatoes, wine, red pepper flakes, oregano, basil, thyme, ½ teaspoon salt, and several grinds of pepper and stir to combine. Bring to a boil, reduce the heat, and simmer until the flavors have blended and the liquid has slightly reduced, about 20–25 minutes. Taste and adjust the seasoning, if necessary.

# pizza remixes

*each recipe makes 2 to 4 servings*

## margherita

1 heirloom tomato, thinly sliced

4 oz (125 g) fresh mozzarella cheese, drained and torn

1 cup (8 fl oz/250 ml) balsamic vinegar

Handful of fresh basil leaves

Preheat the oven and prep the dough (page 52). Arrange the tomato slices and scatter the mozzarella on top. Bake until the crust is golden and the cheese starts to bubble and brown, about 15 minutes.

While the pizza is baking, make a balsamic reduction. In a saucepan over medium-high heat, bring the balsamic vinegar to a simmer. Simmer for 8–10 minutes, until reduced by about one third. Let cool for several minutes.

Let the pizza rest briefly. Slice into triangles, drizzle with the balsamic, top with the basil, and serve warm.

## fontina, mushrooms & thyme

1 tablespoon olive oil

1 clove garlic, minced

8 oz (250 g) mixed mushrooms, such as cremini, porcini, and oyster, cut into bite-size pieces

1 tablespoon chopped fresh thyme leaves

1/4 cup (2 fl oz/60 ml) premade fresh Alfredo sauce

1 cup (4 oz/125 g) shredded fontina cheese

Preheat the oven and prep the dough (page 52). In a sauté pan over medium-high heat, warm the olive oil. Add the garlic and stir until fragrant, about 1 minute. Add the mushrooms and stir until they release their liquid, 5 minutes. Remove from the heat and sprinkle with the thyme and salt. Spread the prepared pizza dough with the Alfredo sauce and sprinkle with the fontina. Arrange about 1/2 cup (2 oz/60 g) of the mushrooms on top, reserving the rest for another use (like in scrambled eggs or on toast). Bake until the crust is golden and the cheese starts to bubble and brown, about 15 minutes. Let the pizza rest briefly, slice into triangles, and serve warm.

## prosciutto, ricotta & arugula

1/4 cup (2 fl oz/60 ml) premade fresh Alfredo sauce

1/2 cup (4 oz/125 g) fresh ricotta cheese

4 thin slices prosciutto, torn

1 cup (1 oz/30 g) arugula

Olive oil for drizzling

Preheat the oven and prep the dough (page 52). Spread the prepared pizza dough with the Alfredo sauce and scatter with pinches of the ricotta. Nestle the prosciutto throughout. Generously grind with pepper. Bake until the crust is golden and the cheese starts to bubble and brown, about 15 minutes. Let the pizza rest briefly. In a bowl, drizzle the arugula with a little olive oil, sprinkle lightly with salt, and toss with your fingers. Slice the pizza into triangles, heap the arugula leaves on top, and serve warm.

## spicy broccoli rabe

1 tablespoon olive oil

2 cloves garlic, minced

1/2 teaspoon red pepper flakes

1 bunch broccoli rabe, chopped

Juice from 1/2 lemon

1/3 cup (3 fl oz/80 ml) Marinara (page 52), or jarred

1 cup (4 oz/125 g) shredded mozzarella cheese

1/4 cup (1 oz/30 g) pitted Kalamata olives

Preheat the oven and prep the dough (page 52). In a sauté pan over medium-high heat, warm the oil. Add the garlic and red pepper flakes and stir until fragrant, 1 minute. Add the broccoli rabe and sauté until bright green and just starting to brown, 5 minutes. Remove from the heat, squeeze the lemon juice over, and sprinkle with salt. Spread the prepared pizza dough with the marinara and sprinkle with the mozzarella. Arrange about 1/2 cup (2 oz/60 g) of the broccoli rabe on top, reserving the rest for another use. Stud with the olives. Bake until the crust is golden and the cheese starts to bubble and brown, about 15 minutes. Let the pizza rest briefly, slice into triangles, and serve warm.

# chapter 3: fish delish
## fish & shellfish

59    oregon niçoise with hot-smoked salmon

60    teriyaki salmon with wasabi noodles

62    tuna-noodle casserole with capers & dill

63    panfried sole with brown butter & capers

65    grown-up fish sticks with yogurt-dill sauce

66    fish tacos with pickled onions & chipotle sauce

68    crab cakes with caesar salad

69    thai-style green curry with prawns

71    vietnamese-style fresh rolls with peanut sauce

72    lobster roll sliders

74    grilled scallops wrapped in bacon

75    jambalaya with prawns & andouille

Hot-smoked salmon is a specialty in the Pacific Northwest, where I grew up. My dad catches big fish, sends them off to the smoker, and a few weeks later we get a box of bricks, studded with peppercorns and spices. The flaked fish adds meaty, smoky flavor to a nouveau salade Niçoise, which is packed with eggs, potatoes, green beans, and the signature briny black olives.

# oregon niçoise with hot-smoked salmon

4 large eggs

Salt and freshly ground pepper

8 small red potatoes

½ lb (250 g) green beans

5 oz (155 g) mixed greens

1 lb (500 g) hot-smoked salmon

16 Niçoise olives

16 cherry tomatoes, halved lengthwise

Aioli for serving (optional)

for the balsamic vinaigrette

2 tablespoons Dijon mustard

2 tablespoons balsamic vinegar

½ cup (4 fl oz/125 ml) extra-virgin olive oil

*makes 4 servings*

Put the eggs in a saucepan and add enough cold water to cover by a couple of inches. Bring to a boil, remove from the heat, cover, and let rest for 20 minutes. Drain the eggs and rinse under cold water. When cool enough to handle, peel and quarter the eggs lengthwise.

While the eggs are cooling, refill the saucepan with salted water and bring to a boil. Add the potatoes and cook until tender when pierced with the tip of a knife, 8–10 minutes. Using a slotted spoon, transfer the potatoes to a colander and rinse under cold water. When cool enough to handle, cut the potatoes in half. Add the green beans to the boiling water and cook just until bright green and tender-crisp, 2 minutes. Drain the green beans and rinse under cold water.

To make the balsamic vinaigrette, in a jar, combine the mustard, balsamic vinegar, olive oil, ½ teaspoon salt, and several grinds of pepper. Shake to combine. Taste and adjust the seasoning, if necessary. Put the greens in a large bowl. Pour half of the dressing over the greens and toss to coat. Taste a leaf and add more dressing as needed, and save any remaining for another use.

Divide the dressed greens between 4 plates. Top with the salmon, eggs, potatoes, green beans, olives, and tomatoes, dividing and arranging them on the greens. Dollop aioli on the side, if you like, grind with pepper, and serve.

Shopping Tip: When shopping for fish, the best advice is always to shop fresh, wild, and in season. We're all on a budget, but personally, I avoid farmed Atlantic salmon, which isn't great for the environment, and doesn't taste great, either. I often buy Coho, which tends to be more affordable. Splurge on Chinook or King, the reigning monarch of salmon, for a special occasion.

*Nearly everybody—from kids to adults to the fish suspicious—loves teriyaki salmon. It hits that trifecta of sweet, savory, and umami. Plate salmon alongside steamed rice and veggies for a quick weeknight meal. Or go big with fatty udon noodles, drenched in a murky, spicy sauce.*

# teriyaki salmon with wasabi noodles

for the salmon

¼ cup (2 fl oz/60 ml) soy sauce

¼ cup (2 fl oz/60 ml) Mirin (see page 10)

2 tablespoons rice vinegar

2 tablespoons firmly packed brown sugar

1 teaspoon grated fresh ginger

1½ lb (750 g) salmon fillet

for the wasabi noodles

1 tablespoon wasabi paste

2 tablespoons soy sauce

2 tablespoons sesame oil

Salt

10 oz (315 g) dried udon noodles

2 green onions, white and pale green parts only, chopped

Black sesame seeds for sprinkling

*makes 4 servings*

To make the salmon, in a small baking pan, add the soy sauce, Mirin, rice vinegar, brown sugar, and ginger and whisk with a fork. Add the salmon, turning to coat. Marinate for 15–30 minutes, turning once or twice.

Preheat the oven to 400°F (200°C). Line a baking sheet with foil and place the salmon, skin down, on the prepared sheet. Bake until the salmon is nearly firm to the touch and flakes easily when pierced with a fork, 15–20 minutes, depending on the thickness of the fish. It should still be a little pink at the thickest part.

While the fish is baking, make the wasabi noodles. In a small bowl, add the wasabi, soy sauce, and sesame oil and whisk with a fork. Bring a large pot full of salted water to a boil. Add the udon noodles and cook until tender, according to package directions. Drain the noodles, return to the pot, and toss with the wasabi sauce and the green onions.

Heap the noodles onto plates and place pieces of salmon on the side. Sprinkle with sesame seeds and serve warm.

Cooking Tip: For nearly all fish, the key is to avoid overcooking it. For the best results, pull the salmon from the oven when it's just shy of firm when pressed, and still nice and juicy.

Remember tuna-noodle casserole? Set down that can of soup! This is my refresh of the retro classic, completely from scratch, and brightened with dry white wine, tart capers, and a whiff of dill. It still bubbles in the oven to create that comforting breadcrumb crust. Based on personal experience, making a big batch will endear you to siblings and roommates, who never seem to have any trouble sniffing out leftovers tucked away in the fridge.

# tuna-noodle casserole with capers & dill

**Salt and freshly ground pepper**

**1 lb (500 g) dried rotini, farfalle, or conchiglie pasta**

**Olive oil for drizzling**

**2 tablespoons unsalted butter**

**2 tablespoons all-purpose flour**

**1 cup (8 fl oz/250 ml) chicken stock, warmed**

**1 cup (8 fl oz/250 ml) dry white wine**

**1 cup (8 oz/250 g) sour cream, light or regular**

**Juice of 1 lemon**

**1 large can (12 oz/375 g) or 2 regular cans (5 oz/155 g *each*) albacore tuna in water, drained**

**¼ cup (2 oz/60 g) capers**

**1 teaspoon dried dill**

**¼ cup (1 oz/30 g) dried breadcrumbs**

**¼ cup (1 oz/30 g) freshly grated Parmesan cheese**

**Paprika for dusting**

*makes 8 servings*

Preheat the oven to 350°F (180°C). Butter a large casserole pan.

Bring a large pot full of salted water to a boil. Cook the rotini according to package directions, stopping 1 minute before the shortest suggested time. Drain, rinse with cold water, and return to the pot. Drizzle with olive oil, toss, and set aside.

While the pasta is cooking, in a saucepan over medium heat, melt the butter. Add the flour, whisk to combine, and let bubble for 30 seconds. Slowly pour in the stock and wine and whisk frequently until thick, 10 minutes. Remove from the heat and add the sour cream, lemon juice, 1 teaspoon salt, and a generous grind of pepper and stir to combine.

Pour the sauce over the pasta, add the tuna, capers, and dill, and stir to combine. Scrape the tuna-noodle mixture into the prepared pan. Sprinkle with the breadcrumbs and Parmesan and dust lightly with paprika.

Bake until golden and bubbling, 30–35 minutes. Spoon the casserole into bowls, grind with pepper, and serve warm.

When it comes to thin, delicate sole fillets, my advice is: the more butter, the better. The butter will foam up around the fish, then settle and start to turn brown and toasty. A little wine, lemon, and capers swirled in at the end are all you need for a sauce. Slide the fillets next to fluffy mashed potatoes (page 99), spoon plenty of the pan sauce over, and pile some buttered green beans and carrots on the side.

# panfried sole with brown butter & capers

1½ lb (750 g) sole fillets

Salt

3 tablespoons unsalted butter, plus more as needed

1 cup (8 fl oz/250 ml) dry white wine

Juice of 1 lemon

2 tablespoons capers

*makes 4 servings*

Preheat the oven to low (200°F/95°C). Sprinkle the sole on both sides with salt. In a large nonstick frying pan over medium-high heat, melt 2 tablespoons of the butter, enough to generously coat the bottom of the pan. Working in batches, fry the sole, turning once, until it's nearly firm and flakes easily when pierced with a fork, 2 minutes per side, depending on the thickness of the fish. Transfer the cooked sole to plates and keep warm in the oven. Add more butter to the pan as needed between batches.

When all of the sole is finished, return the pan to the stove and reduce the heat to low. Add the wine, lemon juice, and capers and swirl to combine. Simmer until reduced by about half. Remove from the heat, add 1 tablespoon butter, and whisk until melted and glossy.

Remove the plates from the oven, spoon the sauce and capers over the sole, and serve warm.

Tools Tip: Most people use nonstick cookware for anything and everything, which isn't really necessary (see page 8). But with tender sole, it's definitely a good idea. Grab your best nonstick pan and a wide spatula to help keep the flaky fish from falling apart. But don't get worked up if it does. It'll still be delicious.

This is my reimagining of the kid classic, focusing on the highlights—firm white fish, a crispy, golden exterior, and plenty of dipping sauce. I like yogurt brightened with fresh herbs and lemon, but you can grab a jar of tartar sauce or ketchup, if you're feeling old school. The fish isn't technically "sticks." Each serving is a big hunk of fillet, more like pub fish and chips. Plate with oven fries, peas, and a pint. Not-so-kid dinner is served.

# grown-up fish sticks with yogurt-dill sauce

for the dipping sauce

1 cup (8 oz/250 g) plain yogurt

1 small shallot, minced

Grated zest and juice of ½ lemon

¼ cup (⅓ oz/10 g) fresh dill, minced

Salt and freshly ground pepper

Canola oil cooking spray

4 serving-size fillets cod or halibut (about 1½ lb/750 g total)

½ cup (2½ oz/75 g) all-purpose flour

2 large eggs

2 cups (3 oz/90 g) panko breadcrumbs

makes 4 servings

To make the dipping sauce, in a small bowl, add the yogurt, shallot, lemon zest and juice, dill, ¼ teaspoon salt, and a generous grind of pepper and stir to combine. Taste and adjust the seasoning, if necessary. Cover and refrigerate until ready to serve.

Preheat the oven to 400°F (200°C). Line a large baking sheet with foil and spray generously with the oil.

Lightly sprinkle the cod on both sides with salt. Pour the flour onto a plate. Crack the eggs into a shallow bowl and whisk with a fork. Pour the breadcrumbs onto another plate. Line up the fish, flour, eggs, breadcrumbs, and prepared baking sheet on the counter.

Working with one piece of cod at a time, dredge in the flour, gently shaking off any excess. Dip into the beaten eggs, letting any excess drip back into the bowl. Coat with the breadcrumbs, pressing gently to help them stick. Repeat with all of the cod, spacing the coated pieces on the baking sheet at the end. Spray over the top with oil.

Bake until the breadcrumbs are golden and the cod is nearly firm to the touch and flakes easily when pierced with a fork, about 12–15 minutes, depending on the thickness of the fish.

Transfer the fish to plates, sprinkle with salt, dollop dipping sauce on the side, and serve warm.

*I live in California, land of fish tacos, and these are quintessentially fresh, flavorful, and laid back. Just flake some firm white fish and load it onto pillowy tortillas with all your favorite toppings. Pickled onions add vinegary crunch, and a drizzle of smoky chipotle sauce will leave guests licking their fingers. Serve with a light Mexican beer, with a lime wedge squeezed in the neck. Charred corn (page 140) would be a delicious side.*

# fish tacos with pickled onions & chipotle sauce

**for the pickled onions**

**1½ cups (12 fl oz/375 ml) white vinegar**

**Juice of 1 lime**

**2 tablespoons sugar**

**Salt**

**1 small red onion, thinly sliced and separated into rings**

**for the chipotle sauce**

**½ cup (4 oz/125 g) crema (see page 10) or sour cream**

**Juice of ½ lime**

**½ teaspoon ground chipotle, or 1 tablespoon canned chipotle in adobo sauce (see page 10)**

**½ teaspoon paprika**

**1 lb (500 g) white fish fillets, such as snapper, tilapia, or mahi mahi**

**Juice of 1 lime**

**2 tablespoons olive oil**

**Chile powder for sprinkling**

**Ground cumin for sprinkling**

**for serving**

**8–12 small corn or flour tortillas**

**Thinly sliced green cabbage**

**Diced avocado or guacamole (page 124)**

**Fresh cilantro leaves**

*makes 4 servings*

To make the pickled onions, in a small bowl, add the vinegar, lime juice, sugar, and 1 teaspoon salt and stir until the sugar has dissolved. Add the onion rings, packing them in gently until immersed in the brine. Soak for about 1 hour. Drain and transfer to a bowl. Cover and refrigerate until ready to serve.

To make the chipotle sauce, in a small bowl, add the crema, lime juice, chipotle, paprika, and a pinch of salt and whisk with a fork to combine. Cover and refrigerate until ready to serve.

Place the fish in a small baking dish, drizzle with the lime juice and olive oil, and turn to coat. Sprinkle lightly on both sides with chile, cumin, and salt. Marinate for 30 minutes.

Preheat a grill pan or cast-iron skillet over medium-high heat. Working in batches if necessary, add the fish and cook until it's nearly firm to the touch and flakes easily when pierced with a fork, about 3 minutes per side, depending on the thickness of the fish. Transfer to a plate and flake with a fork.

Whisk the chipotle sauce to recombine. Set out the pickled onions, chipotle sauce, tortillas, cabbage, avocado, and cilantro. Place 2 or 3 tortillas on each plate, pile the flaked fish on top, and serve warm, letting guests load with their favorite toppings at the table.

Prep Tip: This recipe consists of three easy steps, and if you're having friends over, you can make most of it ahead. Both the pickled onions and the chipotle sauce can be made in advance, covered, and refrigerated until guests turn up.

... these are quintessentially fresh, flavorful, and laid back.

*Tender herb-flecked crab cakes are an uncomplicated treat, especially when they're tucked alongside a classic Caesar salad. The raw egg yolks in the dressing make it extra buttery and delicious, but if you prefer, you can substitute ¼ cup (2 fl oz/60 ml) of mayo for the yolks. Round out the menu with warm sourdough, sweet butter, and a smooth microbrew.*

# crab cakes with caesar salad

for the crab cakes

**1 large egg, lightly beaten**

**¼ cup (2 fl oz/60 ml) mayo**

**Juice of ½ lemon**

**1 tablespoon Worcestershire sauce**

**½ teaspoon paprika**

**Salt and freshly ground pepper**

**1 lb (500 g) fresh lump crabmeat, picked over for shells**

**½ cup (2 oz/60 g) dried breadcrumbs**

**2 tablespoons minced fresh parsley leaves**

**2 tablespoons olive oil, or as needed**

for the caesar salad

**1 clove garlic, mashed to a paste**

**2 large egg yolks**

**2 tablespoons fresh lemon juice**

**1 teaspoon Dijon mustard**

**1 teaspoon Worcestershire sauce**

**½ teaspoon anchovy paste**

**½ cup (4 fl oz/125 ml) extra-virgin olive oil**

**1 or 2 heads romaine lettuce, chopped**

**½ cup (2 oz/60 g) shaved Parmesan cheese**

*makes 4 servings*

To make the crab cakes, in a large bowl, add the egg, mayo, lemon juice, Worcestershire, paprika, a pinch of salt, and several grinds of pepper and whisk to combine. Add the crab and sprinkle with the breadcrumbs and parsley. Mix gently to combine. Gently shape the mixture into 8 cakes. Place on a clean plate. Line a second plate with paper towels, and set near the stove.

Preheat the oven to low (200°F/95°C). In a large nonstick frying pan over medium-high heat, warm the oil. Working in batches if necessary, fry the crab cakes until crispy and golden, turning once, about 3 minutes per side. Transfer to the paper towels to drain. Sprinkle with salt. Keep warm in the oven until ready to serve. Add more oil to the pan as needed between batches.

To make the Caesar salad, in a jar, combine the garlic, egg yolks, lemon juice, mustard, Worcestershire, anchovy paste, ¼ teaspoon salt, several grinds of pepper, and the olive oil. Shake to combine. Taste and adjust the seasoning, if necessary. Put the romaine in a large bowl. Pour half of the dressing over the romaine, and toss to coat. Taste a leaf and add more dressing as needed, and save any remaining for another use.

Divide the salad between plates and place a couple of crab cakes on the side. Sprinkle the salads with the Parmesan, grind with pepper, and serve.

Tools Tip: Crumbly crab cakes are a good reason to pull out a nonstick pan (see page 8). Keep the surface coated with oil, enough to maintain a steady sizzle, to help the crab cakes release easily.

Thai takeout is my guilty pleasure—after a rough week at work, all I want to do is eat curry on the couch, while watching a ridiculous rom-com. But the reality is that most Thai curries are just a handful of quick-cooking ingredients slipped into a fragrant broth. Tender prawns and fresh veggies suit the delicate flavors of lemongrass and jasmine rice.

# thai-style green curry with prawns

1 can (15 fl oz/465 ml) coconut milk

1 cup (8 fl oz/250 ml) water or vegetable stock

Juice of 1/2 lime

1 tablespoon fish sauce (see page 10)

1 tablespoon firmly packed brown sugar

3 tablespoons green curry paste (see page 10)

1 tablespoon grated fresh ginger

2-inch (5-cm) piece lemongrass, lightly crushed

1 small zucchini, thickly sliced

1 small Japanese eggplant, halved lengthwise and thickly sliced

1/2 red bell pepper, seeded and thinly sliced

1 small can (8 oz/250 g) bamboo shoots, drained

8 oz (250 g) large shrimp, peeled and deveined

Handful of fresh basil leaves, preferably Thai, torn

Steamed jasmine rice for serving

makes 4 servings

In a pot over medium-high heat, add the coconut milk, water, lime juice, fish sauce, brown sugar, curry paste, and ginger and stir to combine. Tuck in the lemongrass. Reduce the heat and simmer to let the flavors blend, 5 minutes.

Add the zucchini, eggplant, bell pepper, and bamboo shoots and simmer until the eggplant is just shy of tender, 5 minutes. Add the shrimp and cook until bright pink and curled, 2 minutes longer. Remove from the heat and stir in the basil.

Heap the rice into bowls, spoon the curry on top, and serve warm.

Shopping Tip: Curry paste (see page 10) is amazingly high impact, adding big flavor by the spoonful. Look for it in small jars, among other Asian ingredients at the grocery store. It comes in red and green and other varieties, and it's a great base, but it gets even better with fresh ginger and herbs.

My friend Karen introduced me to the beauty of the Vietnamese fresh roll. So-called spring or summer rolls can include all kinds of thinly slivered veggies, leafy herbs like cilantro and mint, and fresh seafood like prawns, crab, or lobster. Package it all up in a rice wrapper for dunking in an addictive peanut sauce.

# vietnamese-style fresh rolls with peanut sauce

**for the peanut sauce**

1/4 cup (2 1/2 oz/75 g) **unsweetened peanut butter**

1/4 cup (2 fl oz/60 ml) **hoisin (see page 10)**

1 tablespoon **soy sauce**

1 tablespoon **Sriracha sauce (see page 10)**

2 tablespoons **rice vinegar**

1 teaspoon **sugar**

1 oz (30 g) **dried rice vermicelli**

8 **lettuce leaves**

1/4 **cucumber, seeded and cut into matchsticks**

1 **carrot, cut into matchsticks**

1/2 **bell pepper, seeded and cut into matchsticks**

1/4 cup (1/4 oz/7 g) **fresh cilantro, mint, or basil leaves**

16 **large shrimp, cooked, peeled, deveined, and halved lengthwise**

8 **dried rice-paper wrappers**

*makes 4 servings*

To make the peanut sauce, in a small bowl, add the peanut butter, hoisin, soy sauce, Sriracha, vinegar, and sugar and whisk with a fork. Set aside until ready to serve.

Soak the vermicelli in hot water until tender, according to package directions. Drain and return to a small bowl. Wash and dry the lettuce leaves and prep the cucumber, carrot, bell pepper, herbs, and shrimp. Line up all of the ingredients on the counter with a work surface at the end.

Fill a large bowl with warm water. Working with one rice-paper wrapper at a time, dip it into the water for a few seconds, and place the moistened wrapper on the work surface. (The wrapper will continue to soften as it sits.) Arrange the vermicelli, lettuce, cucumber, carrot, and bell pepper in a line on top of the wrapper. Sprinkle with the herbs. Lay a couple of shrimp on top. Gently but firmly roll up the rice wrapper around the filling, tucking in the ends like a burrito. Repeat with the remaining wrappers and filling.

Stack the fresh rolls on plates and serve, passing the peanut sauce at the table. The rolls can also be prepared 1 or 2 hours ahead and covered with plastic wrap or a damp paper towel and refrigerated until ready to serve.

Prep Tip: Soak rice-paper wrappers until just pliable, but not floppy. Wrap only as many rolls as you plan to eat tonight. If you're feeding a crowd, set out piles of ingredients on a board, and have your friends help wrap and roll.

*Sliders are too cute to resist. Load up mini buns with a creamy lobster salad and watch them disappear. You can substitute 1 lb (500 g) lump crabmeat or bay shrimp, if lobster isn't in the budget this month. It's no lobster, but you still get yummy, summery seafood bites.*

# lobster roll sliders

**1 dried bay leaf**

**6 black peppercorns**

**$1/2$ cup (4 fl oz/125 ml) dry white wine**

**About $1^1/2$ lb (750 g) lobster in the shell, approximately 4 tails and 4 claws (see note)**

**$1/4$ cup (2 fl oz/60 ml) mayo**

**Juice of $1/2$ lemon**

**1 rib celery, finely chopped**

**Pinch of cayenne pepper**

**Salt**

**8 small rolls (light and fluffy, not crusty)**

**Melted butter for brushing**

**Butter lettuce leaves, torn**

*makes 4 servings*

In a saucepan, add the bay leaf, peppercorns, and white wine. Fill halfway with water. Bring to a simmer and adjust the heat to maintain. Add the lobster tails and poach until bright red and curled, about 5 minutes. Remove from the heat and rinse under cold water. When the lobster tails are cool enough to handle, crack the shells and remove the meat. (You can use shellfish crackers, a pair of kitchen shears, or strong scissors to cut along the underside and break apart.) Crack and shell the claws, as well. Roughly chop the meat.

In a large bowl, add the mayo, lemon juice, celery, cayenne, and $1/4$ teaspoon salt and stir to combine. Add the chopped lobster and turn to coat.

Split the rolls down the middle, toast, and brush with the melted butter. Pack the rolls with lobster salad, top each with a few pieces of butter lettuce, and serve.

Shopping Tip: If you live somewhere you can buy a whole cracked and cleaned lobster at the fish counter, one or two whole lobsters would be perfect for this recipe. But, if you're deprived like me, the next best scenario is to get a combo of tails and claws. I recommend 4 tails and 4 claws, to get a good mix, but the goal is to hit at least $1^1/2$ lb (750 g) of lobster in the shell. I trust you to do the math. The tails typically come raw, so you'll need to poach those. The claws usually come cooked, so you can just get cracking!

*Almost everything is better wrapped in bacon. But sweet and briny sea scallops just might be my all-time favorite. Bundle up the milky shellfish, thread them onto skewers, and fire up the grill. The bacon crisps, the scallops plump, and the whole package steeps in smoke. Serve with garlic bread (page 140) and asparagus, or any other favorite grilled veggies.*

# grilled scallops wrapped in bacon

Juice of ½ lemon

1 tablespoon olive oil

2 cloves garlic, minced

Salt and freshly ground pepper

20 large sea scallops
(about 1½ lb/750 g total)

10 thin slices bacon

*makes 4 servings*

In a small baking pan, add the lemon juice, olive oil, garlic, a pinch of salt, and a generous grind of pepper and whisk with a fork. Add the scallops and turn to coat. Marinate, turning occasionally, for about 30 minutes.

While the scallops are marinating, preheat the grill or a grill pan to medium-high heat. If you're working with charcoal, when the coals are gray at the edges, rake them across two-thirds of the bottom in a thick layer. Oil the grill rack.

Cut the slices of bacon in half crosswise. Lay a piece of bacon on a cutting board, place a marinated scallop at one end, and roll it up into a snug bundle. The bacon should overlap just enough to stay secure. Thread the bacon-wrapped scallop onto a skewer. Repeat with the remaining scallops and bacon, loading 4 or 5 scallops to a skewer.

Grill until the scallops are nearly firm and the bacon is crisp and marked, about 5 minutes per side. Transfer to plates and serve warm.

Jambalaya is a big pot packed with tempting prawns, chicken, and sausage. The signature Cajun flavor emerges from that slow-simmered tomato sauce, redolent with garlic, peppers, and paprika. And with rice plumping right in the mix, no side dishes are necessary.

# jambalaya with prawns & andouille

1 tablespoon olive oil

8 oz (250 g) andouille sausage, thickly sliced

1 yellow onion, chopped

2 ribs celery, chopped

1 red bell pepper, seeded and chopped

2 cloves garlic, minced

1 teaspoon paprika

1/2 teaspoon *each* dried oregano, dried thyme, cayenne pepper

1 1/2 cups (10 1/2 oz/330 g) long-grain white rice

1 can (15 oz/470 g) diced tomatoes

1 tablespoon tomato paste

1 cup (8 fl oz/250 ml) chicken stock

1 dried bay leaf

1 1/2 cups (9 oz/280 g) cooked shredded chicken

8 oz (250 g) large shrimp, shell on (see note)

Salt and freshly ground pepper

makes 8 servings

In a large Dutch oven over medium-high heat, warm the oil. Add the sausage and cook until browned, about 10 minutes. Transfer to a plate and set aside.

Return the pot to the heat and add the onion, celery, and pepper and sauté until tender, 5 minutes. Add the garlic, paprika, oregano, thyme, and cayenne and stir until fragrant, 1 minute. Add the rice and stir to coat. Add the tomatoes, tomato paste, and stock. Tuck in the bay leaf. Cover the pot and reduce the heat to low. Simmer until the rice is just shy of tender, 20 minutes or according to package directions.

Add the sausage, chicken, and shrimp and stir to combine. Remove from the heat, cover tightly with a lid, and let rest until all of the ingredients are heated through and the shrimp are bright pink and curled, 5 minutes. Taste and adjust the seasoning, if necessary (the sausage and stock may add enough salt already).

Spoon the jambalaya into bowls, grind with pepper, and serve warm.

Shopping Tip: Shrimp shells are tedious to some people, but they definitely enhance seafood stocks and sauces like this one. If you don't like the fuss, look for "easy-peel" shrimp in the freezer aisle, or at the very least, make sure you keep those tails on!

# chapter 4: winner chicken dinner
## *chicken & turkey*

79    herb roasted chicken

80    panfried chicken breasts with mustard & capers

82    braised chicken thighs with mushrooms & white wine

83    retro chicken & broccoli casserole

85    chicken pot pie with puff pastry

86    masala-style chicken curry

88    pumpkin chicken curry

89    existential ramen with chicken & eggs

91    portland-style chicken bento

92    cowboy chicken salad with cilantro-lime dressing

94    chicken enchiladas with black beans & veggies

95    turkey mole with new world veggies

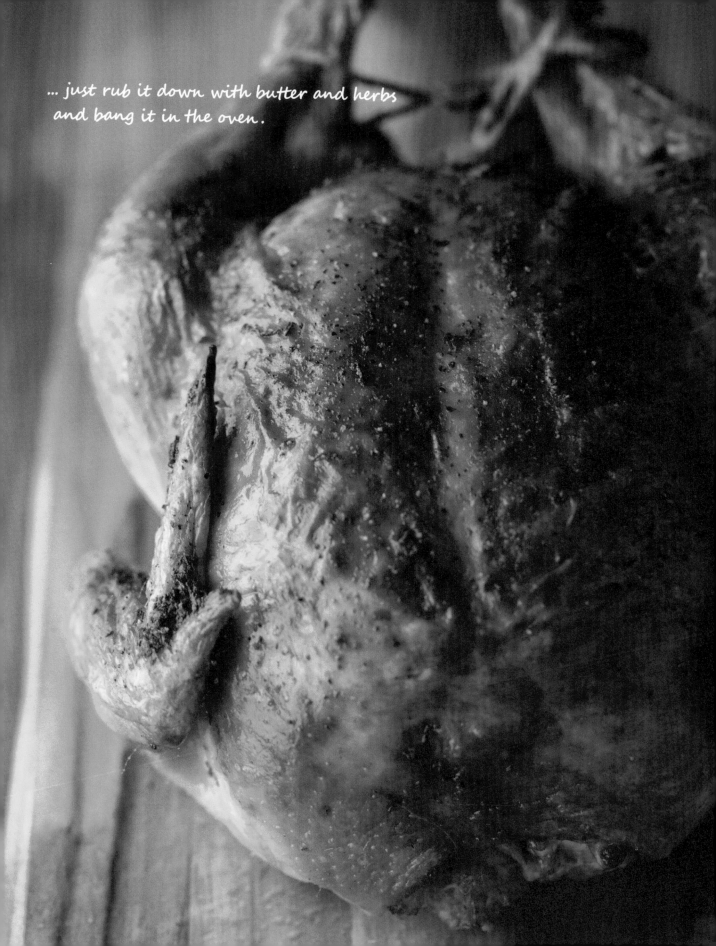

... just rub it down with butter and herbs and bang it in the oven.

Roasting a whole chicken might sound daunting, but it's actually incredibly easy: rub it down with butter and herbs and bang it in the oven. Plus, it's always cheaper to buy a whole chicken than cut-up pieces. Just make sure to open a window and get the kitchen fan going—small apartments can have sensitive smoke alarms. Combining high heat, butter, and a chubby chicken tends to produce a bit of smoke, but don't let that deter you. Delectably crispy skin is worth waving some magazines around.

# herb roasted chicken

1 whole chicken, about 4–5 lb (2–2.5 kg)

Salt and freshly ground pepper

for the herb butter

2 tablespoons unsalted butter, at room temperature

2 tablespoons mixed fresh herbs, such as thyme, oregano, and marjoram leaves

Grated zest of 1 lemon

makes 4 to 6 servings

A few hours ahead or up to the night before, set out a roasting pan or a 9-by-13-inch (23-by-33-cm) baking pan and place a v-shaped rack inside, if you have one. Pat the chicken dry with paper towels and place on the rack or directly in the pan. Sprinkle the chicken all over with salt, inside and out. Cover and refrigerate.

Preheat the oven to 450°F (230°C). Pull the chicken out of the fridge and let it come to room temperature on the counter. To make the herb butter, in a small bowl, add the butter, herbs, lemon zest, ½ teaspoon salt, and a generous grind of pepper and mash with a fork. Slip your fingers under the chicken skin, gently loosening the skin from the meat. Massage the herb butter between the skin and the meat, over the breasts, thighs, and drumsticks, as far as you can reach without tearing the skin. (If that sounds like too much bother, just rub the herb butter all over the bird, putting plenty on the breast.) Season the chicken all over with salt and pepper. If you like, take a short piece of kitchen twine, and tie the legs together (but again, you don't have to).

Roast the chicken until golden and crispy, about 1 hour and 15 minutes, depending on the size of the bird, until a drumstick feels loose in the joint when you wiggle it, and the juices run clear when you pierce a thigh with a paring knife. Transfer the chicken to a cutting board and let rest for 10 minutes.

Carve the chicken into breasts, wings, drumsticks, and thighs. Place one or two pieces on each plate and serve warm.

Prep Tip: Sprinkling the chicken inside and out with salt is a restaurant trick that helps by giving it a mini brine before roasting. That means extra juicy meat and savory skin. You can do this a few hours ahead, or even the night before, which is helpful on busy weeknights. But if you forget, don't worry about it. Your chicken will still be buttery and delicious.

Learning to dredge a chicken breast in breadcrumbs and panfry it until golden is one of those fundamental cooking skills that will always stand you in good stead. I add a swipe of spicy mustard, a big squeeze of lemon, and a spoonful of capers for a flavor lift. Serve with creamy mashed potatoes (page 99), and don't hesitate to dribble the pan juices over everything.

# panfried chicken breasts with mustard & capers

**4 skinless, boneless chicken breasts**

**2 cups (8 oz/250 g) dried breadcrumbs**

**¼ cup (2 oz/60 g) Dijon mustard**

**Salt and freshly ground pepper**

**Olive oil for frying**

**1 tablespoon unsalted butter**

**Juice of 1 lemon**

**¼ cup (2 oz/60 g) capers**

*makes 4 servings*

Place the chicken breasts between two sheets of plastic wrap on a cutting board. Using a meat pounder or rolling pin, pound to an even thickness. Remove and discard the plastic.

Pour the breadcrumbs onto a plate. Place a clean plate next to it. Spread the mustard all over both sides of the chicken. Season generously with salt and pepper. Working with one piece of chicken at a time, coat it with the breadcrumbs, pressing gently to help them stick. Repeat with all of the chicken, stacking the coated pieces on the clean plate at the end.

Preheat the oven to low (200°F/95°C). In a large nonstick frying pan over medium-high heat, warm several tablespoons of olive oil, enough to generously coat the bottom of the pan. Working in batches, fry the chicken, turning once, until golden brown, about 8 minutes per side. Continue to cook until firm and no longer pink at the center. Transfer the cooked chicken to a baking dish, sprinkle with salt, and keep warm in the oven. Add more oil to the pan as needed between batches.

When all of the chicken is finished, return the pan to the stove and reduce the heat to low. Add the butter, lemon juice, and capers to the pan and swirl until the butter is melted and the capers are warmed through, 3 minutes.

Slice the chicken, if you like, and transfer to plates. Spoon the pan sauce and capers over and serve warm.

Prep Tip: Skinless, boneless chicken breasts are lean and quick cooking. The only trick is that they're fatter at one end than the other. Pound them to an even thickness to ensure that they'll come out of the skillet uniformly crisp and juicy.

RESTAURANT
À TOUTE HEURE

2 œufs
Salade
Fromage
Confiture

Pain c

0.10
40
45
50
55
60
65
70

Banquet
Bifteck d
Jambon d
Saucisse ou Jambon
Choucroute saucisse ou Jambon
Soupe à l'oignon
Serviette

BRASSERIE NATIONALE
e de la Répub

There's no doubt that skinless, boneless chicken breasts have won the popularity contest in supermarkets. But for budget and flavor, you can't beat thighs, and when it comes to slow cooking and simmering, dark meat rules. Try this bistro-inspired preparation, which cooks beautifully in a single sauté pan. Brown the chicken first for flavor, then pour in liquids and braise until succulent. The splash of cream and handful of parsley at the end are classic French touches.

# braised chicken thighs with mushrooms & white wine

2 lb (1 kg) chicken thighs (about 4), bone in and skin on

Salt and freshly ground pepper

1 tablespoon olive oil

8 oz (250 g) mushrooms, sliced or quartered

1 small yellow onion, chopped

1 clove garlic, minced

1 tablespoon all-purpose flour

1 cup (8 fl oz/250 ml) dry white wine

1/4 cup (2 fl oz/60 ml) heavy cream (optional)

Buttered egg noodles for serving

Chopped fresh parsley leaves for sprinkling

*makes 4 servings*

Season the chicken thighs generously on both sides with salt and pepper. In a large sauté pan over medium-high heat, warm the oil. Add the chicken and sear until well browned, about 5 minutes per side. Transfer to a plate and set aside. If necessary, drain some of the fat from the pan, leaving enough to coat the bottom, about 1 tablespoon.

Return the pan to the heat. Add the mushrooms and sauté until they release their liquid, 5 minutes. Add the onion and sauté until tender, 5 minutes. Add the garlic and stir until fragrant, 1 minute. Season lightly with salt and pepper. Sprinkle with the flour, stir to coat, and let cook for 30 seconds. Reduce the heat and pour in the wine, stirring to scrape up any browned bits clinging to the bottom of the pan.

Return the chicken to the pan, along with any juices that have accumulated on the plate. Bring to a simmer and adjust the heat to maintain. Cover the pan and simmer until the chicken is fork-tender, about 20 minutes. Remove from the heat and swirl in the cream, if you like.

Heap noodles onto plates and place one or two chicken thighs on the side. Ladle the sauce and mushrooms over everything, sprinkle with parsley, grind with pepper, and serve warm.

Tools Tip: The best pan for the job is a straight-sided sauté pan. If you don't have one of those, just make sure your frying pan is deep enough to hold the liquid.

This is a beloved Duffett family dinner, and I couldn't resist including it. My mom still relies on a favorite Southern recipe from the '80s, and while I cherish it dearly, I'd rather pass on a few processed ingredients. Here's the update, completely from scratch. It's a big pan filled with mouthwatering chicken, tender-crisp broccoli, and a rich, golden sauce. If you've had a rough week at work, take a deep breath and build this casserole. It's the comfort-food solution to all of life's problems.

# retro chicken & broccoli casserole

4 cups (32 fl oz/1 l) chicken stock

1 dried bay leaf

5 or 6 peppercorns

4 skinless, boneless chicken breasts

1 large head broccoli, chopped into bite-size pieces

1 cup (4 oz/125 g) freshly grated Parmesan cheese

$1/4$ cup (2 oz/60 g) unsalted butter

$1/3$ cup (2 oz/60 g) all-purpose flour

1 teaspoon yellow curry powder

1 cup (4 oz/125 g) shredded sharp Cheddar cheese

$1/2$ cup (4 oz/125 g) sour cream

Juice of $1/2$ lemon

Salt and freshly ground pepper

Paprika for sprinkling

Steamed white rice for serving

makes 8 servings

Preheat the oven to 350°F (180°C). In a saucepan, add the stock, bay leaf, and peppercorns. Add enough water to fill halfway. Bring to a simmer and adjust the heat to maintain. Add the chicken breasts and poach until firm and no longer pink at the center, about 10 minutes. Transfer the chicken to a cutting board, and when cool enough to handle, chop into bite-size pieces. Reserve 2 cups (16 fl oz/500 ml) of the stock.

In a 9-by-13-inch (23-by-33-cm) baking pan, spread the broccoli. Sprinkle with about one-third of the Parmesan. Arrange the chicken on top, and sprinkle with another third of the Parmesan.

Wipe out the saucepan. Return the pan to medium heat and melt the butter. Sprinkle with the flour and curry powder, whisk to combine, and let bubble for 30 seconds. Slowly pour in the reserved 2 cups stock and whisk frequently until thick, about 10 minutes. Remove from the heat and add the Cheddar, sour cream, lemon juice, 1 teaspoon salt, and a generous grind of pepper and stir to combine. Taste and adjust the seasoning, if necessary.

Pour the sauce evenly over the broccoli and chicken and sprinkle with the remaining Parmesan. Sprinkle with paprika. Bake until the broccoli is tender and the sauce is bubbling and golden, 30–40 minutes.

Heap the rice into bowls, spoon the casserole over, and serve warm.

This isn't your grandmother's pot pie. Leeks and button mushrooms star, while the classic peas and carrot slices are supporting players. A splash of white wine and a hit of herbs enliven the creamy sauce. Top off the lot with billowy, buttery puff pastry. Premade puff pastry is really good stuff—no kneading involved—and you can find it at a freezer aisle near you! For maximum indulgence, serve with a pint and mash (page 99). As my favorite Englishman would say, "Who ate all the pies?"

# chicken pot pie with puff pastry

1 sheet (14 oz/440 g) frozen puff pastry, thawed

5 tablespoons (2½ oz/75 g) unsalted butter

1 leek, halved lengthwise and sliced (see note)

1 carrot, halved lengthwise and sliced

1 rib celery, sliced

8 oz (250 g) button mushrooms, halved or left whole if small

¼ cup (1½ oz/45 g) all-purpose flour

1 cup (8 fl oz/250 ml) chicken stock, warmed

1 cup (8 fl oz/250 ml) milk, warmed

½ cup (4 fl oz/125 ml) dry white wine

Salt and freshly ground pepper

2 roasted or poached chicken breasts, shredded

1 cup (5 oz/155 g) fresh or frozen peas

1 teaspoon dried thyme

makes 4 servings

Defrost the puff pastry, according to package instructions. (Do not microwave it.) Preheat the oven to 400°F (200°C).

In a sauté pan over medium-high heat, melt 2 tablespoons of the butter. Add the leek, carrot, and celery and sauté until tender, about 5 minutes. Scrape onto a plate and set aside. Return the pan to the heat. Add the mushrooms and sauté until they release their liquid, 5 minutes. Scrape the mushrooms onto the plate with the other vegetables and set aside.

Return the pan to the stove, reduce the heat to medium, and melt the remaining 3 tablespoons of butter. Sprinkle with the flour, whisk to combine, and let bubble for 30 seconds. Slowly pour in the stock, milk, and white wine and whisk frequently until thick, 10 minutes. Season with 1 teaspoon salt and a generous grind of pepper.

Return the reserved mushrooms and other vegetables to the pot, add the chicken, peas, and thyme, and stir to combine. Pour the mixture into a 9-inch (23-cm) pie dish. Let cool slightly. Place the thawed puff pastry on top, trim the edge, and crimp to seal. Cut a few vents in the pastry. Place the pie dish on top of a rimmed baking sheet (just in case it bubbles over in the oven).

Bake until the filling is bubbling and the puff pastry is golden, 50–60 minutes or according to package directions. Let rest for a few minutes. Cut the pastry into wedges, ladle the pastry and filling onto plates, and serve warm.

Prep Tip: Leeks grow in layers, and they tend to trap some grit. Make sure to rinse them thoroughly before cooking. Trim off the roots and green leaves, chop up the white and pale green parts, and then swish them in a bowl of cold water. Transfer to a clean towel and pat dry.

My British boyfriend is addicted to Indian food. I used to be ambivalent, but all of that changed when we started dating, and I realized just how saucy, spicy, and comforting curry can be. The first step is to stock up on the right dry spices (see page 10), which will keep for several months in your cabinet. This chicken tastes awesome the next day, and even better the day after that, once the flavors sink in. Reheat it with rice, pack it into a jacket potato (page 27), or wrap and roll your own curry burrito (below).

# masala-style chicken curry

2 tablespoons olive oil

1 yellow onion, chopped

2 cloves garlic, minced

1 tablespoon grated fresh ginger

1 teaspoon ground cumin

1 teaspoon ground coriander

$\frac{1}{2}$ teaspoon ground turmeric

$\frac{1}{4}$ teaspoon fenugreek seeds

$\frac{1}{8}$ teaspoon cayenne pepper

6 whole cloves

1$\frac{1}{2}$ lb (750 g) skinless, boneless chicken thighs, cut into bite-size pieces

Salt

1 can (15 oz/470 g) diced tomatoes

1 cup (8 fl oz/250 ml) chicken stock

$\frac{1}{2}$ cup (4 fl oz/125 ml) coconut milk (optional)

Steamed basmati rice for serving

Warmed peas for serving

makes 6 servings

In a Dutch oven over medium-high heat, warm the oil. Add the onion and sauté until tender, about 5 minutes. Add the garlic and ginger and stir until fragrant, 1 minute. Add the cumin, coriander, turmeric, fenugreek, cayenne, and cloves and stir until fragrant, 30 seconds.

Add the chicken, stir to coat, and then arrange in a layer on the bottom of the pan. Sprinkle with 1 teaspoon salt. Let the chicken cook for several minutes undisturbed, until it starts to develop a nice brown sear on the bottom. Stir and arrange in a layer again. Cook until the chicken is browned but not cooked through, a few minutes longer.

Add the tomatoes and stock, scraping up any browned bits clinging to the bottom of the pan. Bring to a boil, reduce the heat, and simmer uncovered until the chicken is fork-tender and the liquid has reduced to a thick sauce, 45 minutes. Remove from the heat. Remove and discard the cloves. Stir in the coconut milk, if using.

Heap the rice into bowls, spoon the chicken curry and peas over, and serve warm.

### Curry Hacks: Indian Burritos

This food-truck favorite is a delicious way to repackage leftovers. Ladle chicken curry and basmati rice onto whole-wheat tortillas or naan bread. Top with garbanzo beans and thinly sliced red onion, and drizzle with mint chutney. Roll up like a burrito or fold in half lengthwise and serve warm, or wrap in aluminum foil if you want to take it to go.

This is another Thai-style curry that takes advantage of jarred curry paste for instant flavor and aroma (page 10). Red curry adds a little richness and oomph, to enhance the full flavors and textures of tender chicken and sweet hunks of pumpkin. You can serve it over steamed jasmine rice, but I like red rice even better. It adds pretty color to the plate, and its nuttiness supports the robust sauce.

# pumpkin chicken curry

1 tablespoon canola oil

1 skinless, boneless chicken breast, thinly sliced

2 cloves garlic, minced

1 tablespoon grated fresh ginger

1 small red Thai chile, halved and seeded

2-inch (5-cm) piece lemongrass, lightly crushed

2 tablespoons red curry paste (see page 10)

1 can (15 fl oz/465 ml) coconut milk

Juice of 1/2 lime

2 tablespoons fish sauce (see page 10)

1 tablespoon firmly packed brown sugar

1 small pumpkin (about 2 lb/ 1 kg; see note), peeled, seeded, and cut into bite-size pieces

1/2 red bell pepper, seeded and thinly sliced

Handful fresh basil leaves, preferably Thai, torn

Steamed red rice for serving

*makes 4 servings*

In a Dutch oven over medium-high heat, warm the oil. Add the chicken and sear until just shy of firm, stirring once or twice, 5 minutes. Transfer the chicken to a plate and set aside.

Return the pan to the heat and add the garlic, ginger, chile, and lemongrass and stir until fragrant, 1 minute. Add the curry paste and stir until fragrant, 30 seconds. Add the coconut milk, lime juice, fish sauce, and brown sugar and stir to combine. Add the pumpkin, submerging the pieces in the sauce. Bring to a simmer, reduce the heat to maintain, cover the pot, and cook until the pumpkin is tender when pierced with a fork, 15 minutes.

Return the chicken to the pot, and simmer until firm and no longer pink at the center, 2 minutes. Remove and discard the chile and lemongrass. Remove from the heat and stir in the bell pepper and basil last.

Heap the rice into bowls, spoon the curry over, and serve warm.

Shopping Tip: Your typical jack-o'-lantern only has an inch or two of watery rind, which makes it easy to carve, but disappointing to eat. For cooking, the best pumpkins are small, dense, and fleshy. Look for sugar pie pumpkins or other heirloom varieties, or substitute butternut or acorn squash. The rock star is kabocha, an Asian squash with an exceptionally sweet and fluffy character.

If you don't think you can handle any other recipe in this book, make this ramen, tonight. It cooks in one pot, in under 10 minutes, and it's fragrant and filling. Tender noodles and toothsome chicken nest a poached egg, ready to burst at the poke of a chopstick. But what really takes it over the top is the sensational combination of sesame, Sriracha, and a big handful of fresh herbs. You may never eat packaged ramen ever again.

# existential ramen with chicken & eggs

**4 cups (32 fl oz/1 l) chicken stock**

**1 tablespoon soy sauce**

**Juice of ½ lemon**

**6 oz (185 g) ramen noodles**

**½ cup (3 oz/90 g) cooked shredded chicken**

**2 large eggs**

**Sesame oil for drizzling**

**Sriracha sauce (see page 10) for drizzling**

**Sesame seeds for sprinkling**

**2 handfuls fresh cilantro leaves**

**1 green onion, white and pale green parts only, chopped**

*makes 2 servings*

In a saucepan over medium-high heat, add the stock, soy sauce, and lemon juice and bring to a boil. Add the ramen and cook until tender, according to package directions. Use tongs to divide the noodles between two bowls. Heap the chicken on top of the noodles.

Return the pan with the broth to the stove, bring to a simmer, and reduce the heat to maintain. Crack an egg into a small bowl or ramekin, and gently ease it into the broth (see note). Repeat with the second egg. Cook until the eggs have just set but the yolks are still runny, about 3 minutes.

Using a large slotted spoon, transfer the eggs to the bowls with the noodles, and gently pour in the broth. Drizzle with sesame oil and Sriracha and sprinkle with sesame seeds. Pile the cilantro and green onion on top and serve warm.

Prep Tip: Poaching eggs is not as hard as it seems. Cracking an egg into a small bowl or ramekin gives you a little more control sliding the egg into the simmering broth. Just move slowly, letting the broth flow into the lip of the ramekin, and tilting to ease the egg out. The goal is to help the egg stay together, but even if a few wisps of white float off, it all tastes delicious in your soup.

*I grew up in Portland, Oregon, but—to borrow a hipster line—before it was cool. We didn't have food trucks back in the day, but we did have bento guys. In Japan, bento is any boxed lunch. But in Portland, it's more specific: grilled teriyaki chicken, on a skewer, on a bed of rice, slathered in sticky-sweet chile sauce. If you're doing it right, the chicken has dark grill marks, the onions are charred at the edges, and your backyard smells intoxicating. Throw some zucchini and bell pepper on as well, if you like.*

## portland-style chicken bento

for the teriyaki sauce

½ cup (4 fl oz/125 ml) soy sauce

½ cup (4 fl oz/125 ml) Mirin (see page 10)

¼ cup (2 fl oz/60 ml) rice vinegar

1 tablespoon grated fresh ginger

¼ cup (2 oz/60 g) firmly packed brown sugar

4 skinless, boneless chicken breasts, thickly sliced

1 white onion, cut into big bite-size chunks

Steamed white rice for serving

Sweet chile sauce for serving

*makes 4 servings*

To make the teriyaki sauce, in a glass measuring cup, add the soy sauce, Mirin, vinegar, ginger, and brown sugar and whisk with a fork. Place the chicken in a bowl or baking dish, pour half of the sauce over the chicken, and turn to coat. Cover, refrigerate, and marinate the chicken for 1–4 hours, turning once or twice. Cover and refrigerate the remaining teriyaki sauce until ready to serve.

When the chicken is ready, preheat the grill or a grill pan to medium-high heat. If you're working with charcoal, when the coals are gray at the edges, rake them across two-thirds of the bottom of the grill in a thick layer. Oil the grill rack.

Thread the chicken and onion onto skewers, alternating and starting and ending with chicken. Place the loaded skewers over the hottest part of the grill and cook until well marked, turning once, about 8 minutes per side. Move the skewers to indirect heat, cover the grill, and continue to cook until the chicken is firm and no longer pink at the center.

Heap the rice onto plates and place chicken skewers on the side. Drizzle generously with the reserved teriyaki sauce and the sweet chile sauce and serve warm.

When I'm suffering from carb overload, I turn to this Southwest-style salad. A big bowl of veggies gets rowdy with grilled chicken, black beans, corn, and shredded cheese. It packs enough protein to satisfy cowboys and cowgirls alike. Don't miss out on the fabulously fresh herb dressing, which has a nice kick.

# cowboy chicken salad with cilantro-lime dressing

### for the cilantro-lime dressing

½ cup (½ oz/15 g) loosely packed fresh cilantro leaves

½ jalapeño chile, seeded and chopped

Juice of 2 limes

1 tablespoon agave nectar or honey

⅓ cup (3 fl oz/80 ml) olive oil

Pinch of salt

1 head romaine lettuce, chopped

1 tomato, seeded and chopped

Kernels from 1 cob sweet corn

1 avocado, pitted, peeled, and sliced

½ cup (2½ oz/75 g) oil-packed roasted red pepper, drained and chopped

2 grilled or roasted chicken breasts, chopped

½ cup (3½ oz/105 g) canned black beans, drained and rinsed

½ cup (2 oz/60 g) shredded jack cheese

makes 2 servings

To make the cilantro-lime dressing, in a blender, add the cilantro, chile, lime juice, agave nectar, olive oil, and salt. Pulse until the cilantro is finely chopped but not completely smooth, 10–15 times. Taste and adjust the seasoning, if necessary. Set aside.

In a large bowl, add the romaine, tomato, corn, avocado, red pepper, chicken, beans, and jack and toss to combine. Pour half of the dressing over the ingredients in the bowl, and toss to coat. Taste a leaf and add more dressing as needed, and save any remaining for another use.

Divide the salad between plates, grind with pepper, and serve.

Leftovers Tip: Chopped salads are a great way to use up barbecue chicken (page 139) or roast chicken (page 79). Not hoarding leftovers? Pick up the ultimate convenience food, a whole rotisserie chicken. One bird can feed you for several nights: munch on the drumsticks and wings the first day, chop up the breasts for salads or sandwiches the next, and then shred the thighs for soup or ramen (page 89) later in the week.

Enchiladas are a one-pan comfort, packed with hearty chicken, topped with gooey cheese. I add brown rice, black beans, and sweet corn to make it a full meal. My friend Tricia told me that these are "burrito enchiladas," and insists that real chicken enchiladas only include chicken. If you're also a purist, you can just use shredded chicken for the filling. If you're a vegetarian, substitute chopped roasted veggies. But whatever you do, pile plenty of salsa, guac, and sour cream on top.

## chicken enchiladas with black beans & veggies

1 tablespoon canola oil

½ yellow onion, chopped

3 cloves garlic, minced

1 poblano chile, seeded and chopped

1 teaspoon ground cumin

1 teaspoon chile powder

½ teaspoon dried oregano

2 cups (12 oz/375 g) cooked shredded chicken

1 cup (5 oz/155 g) cooked rice

½ cup (3½ oz/105 g) canned black beans, drained and rinsed

½ cup (3 oz/90 g) frozen or fresh corn kernels

Salt

1 can (28 fl oz/875 ml) green enchilada sauce

8 large flour tortillas

1 cup (4 oz/125 g) shredded jack cheese

for serving

Guacamole (page 124) or sliced avocado

Salsa fresca

Sour cream

makes 8 servings

Preheat the oven to 350°F (180°C). In a large sauté pan over medium-high heat, warm the oil. Add the onion and sauté until tender, about 5 minutes. Add the garlic and poblano and stir until fragrant, 1 minute. Add the cumin, chile powder, and oregano and stir until fragrant, 30 seconds. Remove from the heat. Add the chicken, rice, beans, and corn. Sprinkle with 1 teaspoon salt and stir to combine.

Pour 1 cup (8 fl oz/250 ml) of the enchilada sauce into a large, shallow dish. Line up the tortillas, the enchilada sauce, a 9-by-13-inch (23-by-33-cm) baking pan, and the chicken mixture on the counter. Working with one tortilla at a time, dip it into the sauce, letting any excess drip back into the dish. Transfer to the baking pan, fill with about ½ cup (3 oz/90 g) of the chicken mixture, roll up snugly, and place seam down along a short side of the pan. Continue filling and rolling the tortillas, lining them up to fill the pan. Pour the remaining enchilada sauce over and sprinkle with the jack.

Bake until the sauce is bubbling and the cheese is golden, 30 minutes. Let rest for a few minutes. Separate the enchiladas and transfer to plates. Serve warm, passing the guacamole, salsa, and sour cream at the table.

Mole poblano is a rich combination of nuts, chocolate, and spices, and the premade version is an easy and enticing simmer sauce for poultry. Ground turkey is cheap and flavorful, but you could also use shredded leftover chicken. My friend Elena, Latin American studies major, went on a pre-Columbian veggies kick, sinking succulent squashes, peppers, and corn into the murky mix. Ladle it over fluffy quinoa, and top it off with buttery avocado and fresh cheese.

# turkey mole with new world veggies

1 tablespoon olive oil

¹/₂ yellow onion, chopped

4 cloves garlic, minced

1 teaspoon ground cumin

1 lb (500 g) ground turkey meat, preferably thighs

Salt

1 small zucchini, chopped

1 small summer squash, chopped

1 red bell pepper, seeded and chopped

¹/₂ cup (3 oz/90 g) corn kernels, thawed if frozen

1 box (10 oz/315 g) mole poblano sauce, such as Doña Maria (see note)

1 cup (8 fl oz/250 ml) chicken stock

for serving

Cooked quinoa

Sliced avocado

Sliced tomato

Crumbled cotija cheese

makes 6 servings

In a large sauté pan over medium-high heat, warm the oil. Add the onion and sauté until tender, about 5 minutes. Add the garlic and stir until fragrant, 1 minute. Add the cumin and stir until fragrant, 30 seconds. Add the turkey, breaking it up with a spatula. Sprinkle with ½ teaspoon salt. Let the turkey cook for several minutes undisturbed, until it starts to develop a nice brown sear on the bottom. Stir and break up any larger pieces again. Cook until the turkey is browned and has some crispy edges, a few minutes longer. Transfer to a plate and set aside.

Return the pan to the heat and add the zucchini, squash, pepper, and corn and sauté until tender, 5 minutes. Add the mole sauce and stock, scraping up any browned bits clinging to the bottom of the pan. Return the turkey to the pan. Bring to a boil, reduce the heat, and simmer until the flavors have blended and the sauce has thickened slightly, 10 minutes.

Heap the quinoa into bowls and spoon the mole over. Serve warm, passing the avocado, tomato, and cotija at the table.

Prep Tip: Mole poblano (see page 10) is best when a Mexican *abuela* grinds 20 different spices into a slow-simmered sauce, but you can find the prepared version at any corner bodega and in most grocery stores. It comes in two forms: a paste that needs to be dissolved in hot water or broth, or ready-to-open boxes.

# chapter 5: extra meaty
## beef, pork & lamb

99    porterhouse steak with pan sauce & mash

100   korean barbecue lettuce wraps

103   monday-night meatballs

104   skillet cheeseburgers, cali style

106   school-night beef burritos

107   roasted pork tenderloin with fresh pesto

109   smothered pork chops with sour cream & onions

110   spicy braised sausages & chard with polenta

113   spring greens with lamb, asparagus & fingerling potatoes

114   lamb chops with garlic & rosemary

116   shepherd's pie

117   indian-style lamb & peas

Great steak is sexy and simple, but it all hangs on two crucial elements—really good meat and a really good pan. Porterhouse is my heartthrob: a big T-bone in the center, dividing strip on one side and tenderloin on the other. A lot of salt and a good dab of butter are all it needs. But you could use regular T-bones, strip steaks, or rib eyes, all of which taste like a special occasion without breaking the bank.

# porterhouse steak with pan sauce & mash

for the mashed potatoes

**4 large russet potatoes (2 lb/ 1 kg), peeled and quartered**

**Salt**

**2 tablespoons unsalted butter**

**¼ cup (2 oz/60 g) cream cheese**

**½ cup (4 fl oz/125 ml) milk**

**¼ teaspoon onion powder**

**¼ teaspoon ground white pepper**

**2 lb (1 kg) of your favorite bone-in steak, such as 1 large porterhouse or 2 T-bones, or 1 lb (500 g) of your favorite boneless steak, such as 2 New York strip, thick cut**

**Freshly ground black pepper**

**1 cup (8 fl oz/250 ml) dry red wine**

**1 tablespoon unsalted butter**

*makes 2 generous servings*

To make the mashed potatoes, put the potatoes in a pot, pour in cold water to cover, and salt generously. Bring to a boil and cook until tender when pierced with a fork, 15 minutes. Drain and let steam in the colander for a minute or two. (The drier the potatoes, the fluffier the mash.) Return to the pot. Add the butter and cream cheese and press with a masher or wooden spoon to break up the potatoes. Once the butter and cheese have melted, add the milk, onion powder, white pepper, and 1 teaspoon salt and stir to combine. Taste and adjust the seasoning, if necessary.

Sprinkle the steak(s) generously on both sides with salt and black pepper. Warm a skillet over medium-high heat until good and hot (if you hold your hand an inch above the surface, it should only be comfortable for a few seconds before pulling away). Add the steak and sear, turning once, until medium-rare or done to your liking, about 7 minutes per side, depending on the thickness. Transfer the steak to a cutting board and let rest for 10 minutes. Keep in mind that the steak will continue to cook while it rests.

While the steak is resting, let the skillet cool slightly. Return to low heat and add the wine, scraping up any browned bits clinging to the bottom of the pan. Bring to a simmer and cook until the liquid has reduced slightly, 3 minutes. Remove from the heat and whisk in the butter until glossy.

Heap the mashed potatoes onto plates. Slice the steak and place on the side. Drizzle everything with the pan sauce, grind with pepper, and serve warm.

Tools Tip: The best pan for the job is cast iron, which sears gorgeously. Enameled cast iron would really be best for this recipe, as it won't react with the acid in the wine. But a sturdy stainless steel sauté pan also works. Avoid nonstick—marbled meat doesn't need help releasing from the pan, and the material won't hold up over high heat.

My mouth waters just thinking about bulgogi, Korean-style grilled beef. These fresh and fiery wraps feature caramelized meat, ruffled lettuce leaves, and sticky rice, all drizzled in a spicy chile sauce. It's surprisingly easy to make: just marinate some steak, and sear it in minutes. A barbecue would be best, but on busy weeknights, I pull out my trusty cast-iron pan. Ask the guy at the meat counter to slice the steak very thinly, for tenderness.

# korean barbecue lettuce wraps

for the marinade

¼ cup (2 fl oz/60 ml) soy sauce

1 tablespoon sesame oil

1 tablespoon rice vinegar

1 tablespoon firmly packed brown sugar

2 cloves garlic, minced

1 tablespoon grated fresh ginger

1 lb (500 g) rib eye steak, thinly sliced

Steamed short-grain rice

8 large red-leaf lettuce leaves

Sriracha sauce (see page 10) for drizzling

makes 4 servings

To make the marinade, in a small bowl, add the soy sauce, sesame oil, vinegar, brown sugar, garlic, and ginger and whisk with a fork. Place the steak in a bowl or baking dish, pour the marinade over, and turn to coat. Marinate for 30 minutes, turning once or twice.

Heat a cast-iron skillet or grill pan over medium-high heat until good and hot (if you hold your hand an inch above the surface, it should only be comfortable for a few seconds before pulling away). Working in batches if necessary, add the steak in a single layer and sear, turning once, until well marked, about 3 minutes per side.

Set the steak, rice, lettuce leaves, and Sriracha out on the table. Let guests build their own lettuce wraps. To make a wrap, lay a leaf down on a plate. Place a spoonful of rice at the center, stack with 2 or 3 strips of steak, and drizzle with Sriracha. Gently fold in the sides of the leaf.

*Juicy, well-seasoned meatballs are a comfort and a feast. I make a big batch of these on the weekend and freeze half. (Freeze on a wax paper-lined baking sheet or plate for a few hours, then transfer to a zippered bag). Stagger home on a Monday night, boil some pasta, simmer some marinara, and plunk in a few meatballs to warm through. Dinner is good to go.*

# monday-night meatballs

1 tablespoon olive oil

1/2 small onion, minced

3 cloves garlic, minced

1 lb (500 g) lean ground beef

1 large egg, beaten lightly with a fork

1/2 cup (4 fl oz/125 ml) milk

1/2 cup (2 oz/60 g) dried breadcrumbs

1/2 teaspoon each dried basil, oregano, and thyme

Salt and freshly ground pepper

3/4 lb (375 g) dried linguine or spaghetti

Marinara (page 52), or your favorite jarred

Freshly grated Parmesan for sprinkling

*makes about 18 meatballs; 4 to 6 servings*

Preheat the oven to 400°F (200°C). Oil a large rimmed baking sheet.

In a sauté pan over medium-high heat, warm the oil. Add the onion and sauté until tender, about 5 minutes. Add the garlic and stir until fragrant, 1 minute. Transfer to a large bowl and let cool slightly. Add the beef, egg, milk, breadcrumbs, basil, oregano, thyme, 1 teaspoon salt, and a generous grind of pepper. Gently mix with your hands, just until combined (see note).

Wash and dry your hands. Rub a dab of olive oil between your palms. Take a large pinch of the meat, and roll between your hands until roughly the size and shape of a golf ball. Place on the prepared baking sheet. Continue rolling and spacing the rest of the meatballs. Bake until starting to brown on the bottoms, 12 minutes. Use a spatula to gently loosen and turn the meatballs. Return to the oven and bake until browned on the second side, 5 minutes longer.

While the meatballs are baking, bring a large pot full of salted water to a boil. Add the linguine and cook until al dente, according to package directions. Drain and return to the pot. Drizzle with olive oil, toss, and keep warm. In a large saucepan, bring the marinara to a simmer. When the meatballs are ready, add them to the marinara and turn to coat with the sauce. Simmer to let the flavors blend, a few minutes longer.

Heap the pasta onto plates, top with a few of the meatballs, and ladle marinara over everything. Sprinkle with Parmesan, grind with pepper, and serve warm.

Prep Tip: The only trick is to avoid overmixing the meat, which can toughen it. One of my favorite food bloggers recommends holding your hand kind of like a claw. Imagine that you're an old Italian crone. It's not only entertaining, but also surprisingly effective.

Meatball Hacks: Meatball Sub

Ladle any leftover meatballs and marinara onto **large sandwich rolls**. Sprinkle generously with **shredded mozzarella cheese**. Toast in a toaster oven or low oven until the cheese has melted and the meatballs are warmed through. Smash the sandwiches gently—the smashing really does make it taste better. Cut into halves and serve warm.

Homemade cheeseburgers, straight out of the skillet, are one of my brothers' favorite dinners. You can dress these up with some blue cheese and caramelized onions, or peppered bacon and smoky barbecue sauce, if you like. But the truth is, I like my cheeseburgers In–N–Out style. Super simple, with a soft bun, juicy tomato, crunchy lettuce, and the classic guilty pleasures: American cheese and "special" sauce. Invite over some bros, and serve with cold lager and sweet potato fries.

## skillet cheeseburgers, cali style

1 lb (500 g) lean ground beef

Salt

4 slices American cheese

4 hamburger buns,
preferably brioche

1 large tomato, sliced

4 leaves green lettuce

for the special sauce

½ cup (4 fl oz/125 ml) mayo

2 tablespoons ketchup

2 tablespoons sweet pickle relish

Sweet potato fries for serving

*makes 4 servings*

Gently shape the ground beef into 4 patties about ½ inch (12 mm) thick. Avoid overworking the meat, which will toughen it.

Warm a cast-iron skillet over medium-high heat. Add the patties (they should sizzle on impact). Season generously with salt. Let the patties cook for several minutes undisturbed, until they start to develop a nice brown sear on the bottom. Flip and season the second side with salt. Resist the urge to prod or press the meat. Cook until medium or done to your liking, a few minutes longer. Remove from the heat. Top the burgers with the American cheese, and let rest in the pan until the cheese has melted.

To make the special sauce, in a small bowl, add the mayo, ketchup, and relish and whisk with a fork. Generously spread inside the buns. Stack the buns with the cheeseburgers, tomato, and lettuce, and press gently to seal.

Place the cheeseburgers on plates, pile sweet potato fries on the side, and serve warm.

When I moved into my first apartment, I used to stock up on premade packets of "taco mix." Bad move. Those spice mixes are mostly chile powder, cumin, and dehydrated onions and garlic. Keep the first two in the spice cabinet, use fresh aromatics, and ditch the preservatives. It's cheaper, fresher, and yummier. Seriously. You can sprinkle it over flank steak, chicken breasts, and bell peppers, and throw them on the grill. But on weeknights, I like cheap and comforting ground beef, rolled up with all the fixin's.

# school-night beef burritos

**for the beef filling**

1 tablespoon olive oil

½ yellow onion, finely chopped

4 cloves garlic, minced

2 teaspoons chile powder

1 teaspoon ground cumin

¼ teaspoon cayenne pepper

1 lb (500 g) lean ground beef

Salt

1 tablespoon tomato paste

**for serving**

Canned black beans, drained and rinsed

Flour or corn tortillas

Shredded jack cheese

Diced avocado

Sliced black olives

Chopped romaine

Sour cream

Salsa

makes 4 servings

To make the beef filling, in a large sauté pan over medium-high heat, warm the oil. Add the onion and sauté until tender, about 5 minutes. Add the garlic and stir until fragrant, 1 minute. Add the chile, cumin, and cayenne and stir until fragrant, 30 seconds.

Add the beef, breaking it up with a spatula. Sprinkle with 1 teaspoon salt. Let the beef cook for several minutes undisturbed, until it starts to develop a nice sear on the bottom. Stir and break up any larger pieces again. Cook until the beef is browned and has some crispy edges, a few minutes longer. Reduce the heat to low and add the tomato paste and ⅓ cup (3 fl oz/80 ml) water, stirring to dissolve the tomato paste and scrape up any browned bits clinging to the bottom of the pan. Set aside and keep warm.

Pour the beans into a bowl and warm in the microwave, 1 minute. Wrap the tortillas in a clean kitchen towel and warm in the microwave, 30 seconds. Set the beans, tortillas, jack, avocado, olives, romaine, sour cream, and salsa out on the table.

Divide the tortillas between plates and heap the beef filling and beans on top. Serve warm, letting guests load with their favorite toppings at the table.

A tub of bright basil pesto, freshly made by many groceries and delis, is a helpful pantry staple. In addition to being a 10-minute dinner with pasta (see page 45), it's an instant flavor bomb for pretty much anything, from chicken sandwiches to salad dressing. My boyfriend's mum devised this brilliant combination, which couldn't be simpler—slather pork with a couple of dollops of the good stuff, and roast away. Serve thick slices with fresh corn, creamy polenta, or a big tomato salad.

# roasted pork tenderloin with fresh pesto

**2 small pork tenderloins, about 1⅓–1½ lb (655–750 g) total**

**4 tablespoons (2 fl oz/60 ml) premade fresh basil pesto**

**Olive oil for brushing**

**Salt and freshly ground pepper**

*makes 4 generous servings*

Preheat the oven to 500°F (260°C). Using a sharp knife, slice the pork tenderloins down the center without cutting all the way through. Lay them open and smear 2 tablespoons of the pesto inside each. Fold the halves back together, and tie with kitchen twine or poke with toothpicks in a few places to secure. Brush with olive oil and sprinkle generously with salt and pepper.

Place the pork on a roasting pan or large rimmed baking sheet and roast until nearly firm but still pale pink and juicy at the center, 20–25 minutes. Let rest for 5 minutes. The pork will continue to cook while it rests.

Snip away the strings and carve the pork into thick slices. Transfer to plates and serve warm.

Shopping Tip: Smaller pork tenderloins, about ⅔–¾ lb (330–375 g), tend to be the sweetest and juiciest. You're aiming for 1⅓–1½ lb (655–750 g) total. That should generously feed four people. Think of it as dinner for you, a few friends, and a yummy baguette the next day.

*... even if you overdo it, the savory onion sauce will save you.*

Boneless chops come in convenient portions, and they're as cheap as they are easy. A quick sear followed by a slow braise helps to prevent overcooking and keep the chops plump and juicy. Pressed gently with one finger, a pork chop should feel firm (cooked most of the way through) with just a hint of give (still slightly pink at the center). But even if you overdo it, the savory onion sauce will save you.

## smothered pork chops with sour cream & onions

1/2 cup (2 1/2 oz/75 g) all-purpose flour

4 boneless pork chops, thick cut

Salt and freshly ground pepper

1 tablespoon olive oil

2 tablespoons unsalted butter

1 small onion, halved and thinly sliced

1/2 teaspoon paprika

1 cup (8 fl oz/250 ml) pale ale or dry white wine

1 cup (8 fl oz/250 ml) beef stock

1 teaspoon chopped fresh rosemary leaves

1/2 cup (4 oz/125 g) sour cream

1 tablespoon Worcestershire sauce

Mashed potatoes (page 99) for serving

Chopped fresh parsley leaves for sprinkling

*makes 4 generous servings*

Pour the flour onto a plate. Place a clean plate next to it. Season the pork chops generously with salt and pepper on both sides. Working with one chop at a time, dredge it in the flour, gently shaking off any excess. Repeat with all of the pork, stacking the coated pieces on the clean plate at the end. Reserve 1 tablespoon of the flour.

In a large sauté pan over medium-high heat, warm the oil and butter. When the butter has melted, add the pork chops and sear until browned, turning once, about 3 minutes per side. The pork chops should not be cooked through. Return to the plate and set aside.

Return the pan to the heat. Add the onion and sauté until tender, 5 minutes. Sprinkle with the reserved 1 tablespoon flour and the paprika, stir to coat, and let cook for 30 seconds. Reduce the heat to medium-low and slowly pour in the ale and stock and stir until thickened slightly, 3 minutes. Add the rosemary, sour cream, Worcestershire sauce, 1/2 teaspoon salt, and a generous grind of pepper and stir to combine.

Return the pork chops to the pan, along with any juices that have accumulated on the plate. Turn the pork chops to coat in the sauce. Cover the pan and simmer until the pork chops are nearly firm but still pale pink and juicy at the center, about 10 minutes.

Heap the mashed potatoes onto plates and place the pork chops on the side. Spoon the onions and sauce over everything. Sprinkle with parsley, grind with pepper, and serve warm.

Tools Tip: Just like for chicken thighs (page 82), use a straight-sided sauté pan or deep frying pan, which holds plenty of liquid for braising.

*This is a warming one-pot dinner for chilly days. Thick bites of sausage, dark cooking greens, and lots of tomato and garlic are the basis for a piquant sauce. A bowl of thick and creamy polenta makes a satisfying base to soak up all of the juices.*

# spicy braised sausages & chard with polenta

**1 bunch (about 8 large leaves) Swiss chard**

**2 large spicy sausages, such as linguiça, chorizo, or kielbasa, about 12 oz (375 g) total, thickly sliced**

**2 cloves garlic, minced**

**1/2 teaspoon red pepper flakes**

**Pinch of ground nutmeg**

**Salt and freshly ground pepper**

**1/2 cup (4 fl oz/125 ml) dry red wine**

**1 can (15 oz/470 g) diced tomatoes**

**1 cup (7 oz/220 g) polenta**

**1 tablespoon unsalted butter**

**1/4 cup (1 oz/30 g) freshly grated Parmesan, plus more for sprinkling**

*makes 4 servings*

To prepare the chard, use a paring knife to remove the ribs. Chop the ribs and set aside. Slice the leaves into strips about 2 inches (5 cm) wide and set aside.

In a large sauté pan over medium-high heat, add the sausages and sear until well browned, about 5 minutes per side. Transfer to a plate and set aside. If necessary, drain some of the oil from the pan, leaving enough to coat the bottom, about 1 tablespoon.

Return the pan to the heat. Add the chard ribs and sauté until tender, 5 minutes. Add the garlic, red pepper flakes, nutmeg, 1/2 teaspoon salt, and several grinds of pepper and stir until fragrant, 1 minute. Reduce the heat to low and add the wine, scraping up any browned bits clinging to the bottom of the pan. Add the tomatoes, bring to a simmer, and reduce the heat to maintain. Finally, add the chard leaves and simmer, stirring occasionally, until the leaves have wilted and the liquid has reduced slightly, 10 minutes. Return the sausages to the pan, folding them in with the chard and tomatoes. Taste and adjust the seasoning, if necessary. Keep warm over low heat.

Cook the polenta, stirring frequently, until thick and tender, according to package directions. Remove from the heat and stir in the butter and Parmesan.

Spoon the polenta onto plates and top with the sausages and chard. Sprinkle with Parmesan, grind with pepper, and serve warm.

This is the ultimate springtime salad, lush with peppery greens, tender-crisp asparagus, truffled potatoes, and chewy, flavorful lamb. It's a great way to showcase leftover lamb or steak (page 99). But it's delicious enough that you may want to stop by the meat counter just for this.

# spring greens with lamb, asparagus & fingerling potatoes

for the lamb

1 clove garlic, mashed to a paste

1 tablespoon olive oil

1 lb (500 g) boneless leg of lamb, cut into thick slices (see note)

Salt and freshly ground pepper

for the dressing

2 tablespoons Dijon mustard

2 tablespoons fresh lemon juice

1/2 cup (4 fl oz/125 ml) extra-virgin olive oil

12 small fingerling potatoes

1 teaspoon truffle oil

1 bunch asparagus, cut into bite-size pieces

5 oz (155 g) arugula

1/2 cup (2 oz/60 g) shaved pecorino or Parmesan cheese

makes 4 servings

To make the lamb, in a small bowl, add the garlic and olive oil and stir to make a paste. Place the lamb in a bowl or baking dish and rub all over with the garlic paste. Season generously with salt and pepper. Let rest for 10 minutes.

To make the dressing, in a jar, combine the mustard, lemon juice, olive oil, 1/2 teaspoon salt, and several grinds of pepper. Shake to combine. Taste and adjust the seasoning, if necessary.

Bring a saucepan full of salted water to a boil. Add the potatoes and cook until tender when pierced with the tip of a knife, 8–10 minutes. Using a slotted spoon, transfer the potatoes to a colander and rinse under cold water. When cool enough to handle, cut the potatoes in half, drizzle with the truffle oil, sprinkle with salt, and toss to coat. Add the asparagus to the boiling water and cook just until bright green and tender-crisp, 2 minutes. Drain the asparagus and rinse under cold water. Set aside.

Warm a cast-iron skillet or grill pan over medium-high heat until good and hot (if you hold your hand an inch above the surface, it should only be comfortable for a few seconds before pulling away). Working in batches if necessary, add the lamb in a single layer and sear, turning once, until medium or done to your liking, about 2 minutes per side. Transfer to a cutting board and let rest for a few minutes.

In a large bowl, add the arugula and asparagus. Pour half of the dressing over and toss to coat. Taste a leaf and add more dressing as needed, and save any remaining for another use.

Heap the arugula and asparagus onto plates. Place the potatoes and lamb on the side. Scatter with the pecorino, grind with pepper, and serve.

Shopping Tip: Make friends with your butcher to get the best meat recommendations. You want a cut of lamb that's good for thinly slicing and searing, so avoid shanks (best for braising) or chops (too precious and expensive to hack up). Just ask for a few thick slices of boneless leg meat. Not feeling chatty? Pick up a big New York strip steak, instead.

Tender little lamb chops are too special to mess with much. Rub them down with pungent garlic and woodsy rosemary, and pepper them like you mean it. A quick stint in a hot oven creates a beautiful crust. It's a shame to overcook them—I recommend medium-rare, crusty on the outside, but still pink at the center. Serve with any of your favorite spring veggies, such as new potatoes, baby artichokes, or fresh fava beans.

## lamb chops with garlic & rosemary

**4 or 5 cloves garlic, minced**

**2 tablespoons minced fresh rosemary**

**¼ cup (2 fl oz/60 ml) olive oil**

**2 racks lamb ribs, frenched, 2–3 lbs total (1–1.5 kg)**

**Salt and freshly ground pepper**

*makes 4 to 6 servings*

In a small bowl, add the garlic, rosemary, and olive oil and stir to make a paste. Place the lamb in a baking dish and rub all over with the garlic paste. Season generously with salt and pepper. Cover, refrigerate, and let marinate for several hours.

Preheat the oven to 450°F (230°C). Place the lamb in a roasting pan or on a large rimmed baking sheet. Roast until medium or done to your liking, 20–25 minutes. Transfer the lamb to a cutting board and let rest for 5 minutes. Keep in mind that the lamb will continue to cook while it rests.

Carve between the ribs to separate into chops. Place a few chops on each plate and serve warm.

My mom used to make shepherd's pie when we were little, and I still love it. A succulent stew full of fork-tender lamb is a beautiful thing. But if you dollop some fluffy mashed potatoes on top, scrape them with a fork, and bake until golden and crusty? That's downright cozy. Dig into this on a chilly Sunday night, and then savor the leftovers later in the week.

# shepherd's pie

2 tablespoons olive oil

2 lb (1 kg) lamb stew meat

Salt and freshly ground pepper

1 yellow onion, chopped

2 carrots, chopped

2 celery ribs, chopped

2 cloves garlic, minced

1 tablespoon all-purpose flour

1 cup (8 fl oz/250 ml) dark ale, such as stout or porter

1 cup (8 fl oz/250 ml) beef stock

1 teaspoon Worcestershire sauce

1 tablespoon tomato paste

1 teaspoon dried thyme

Mashed potatoes (page 99)

*makes 6 servings*

In a large Dutch oven over medium-high heat, warm the oil. Add the lamb and arrange in a layer on the bottom of the pan. Sprinkle with 1 teaspoon salt and grind generously with black pepper. Let the lamb cook for several minutes undisturbed, until it starts to develop a nice brown sear on the bottom. Stir and arrange in a layer again. Cook until the lamb is browned but not cooked through, a few minutes longer. Transfer to a plate and set aside.

Return the pan to the heat. Add the onion, carrots, and celery and sauté until tender, 5 minutes. Add the garlic and stir until fragrant, 1 minute. Sprinkle with the flour, stir to coat, and let cook for 30 seconds. Reduce the heat and pour in the ale, stock, Worcestershire sauce, tomato paste, and thyme and stir to combine. Return the lamb to the pan, along with any juices that have accumulated on the plate. Bring to a simmer and adjust the heat to maintain. Cover the pot and simmer, stirring occasionally, until the lamb is nearly tender, about 1 hour.

While the stew is cooking, make the mashed potatoes (page 99).

Preheat the oven to 350°F (180°C). When the stew is ready, remove from the heat and dollop the potatoes evenly over the top. Use a fork to rake the potatoes into ridges. Bake until the potatoes turn golden at the edges, 30 minutes.

Ladle the shepherd's pie into bowls, grind with pepper, and serve warm.

*Between jobs and internships, I've done my share of babysitting, and one of my favorite families taught me this recipe. The kids are crazy for it, and one bite in, I understood why. It's a weeknight cinch, browning quickly in one pan, and rich with caramelized meat, garlic, and cumin. Lamb has big gamy flavor, but if you prefer mellow, use ground beef instead.*

# indian-style lamb & peas

1 tablespoon olive oil

½ yellow onion, finely chopped

4 or 5 cloves garlic, minced

1 tablespoon grated fresh ginger

1½ teaspoons ground cumin

1½ teaspoons ground coriander

Pinch of cayenne pepper

1½ lb (750 g) ground lamb

Salt

1 tablespoon tomato paste

Steamed basmati rice for serving

Warmed peas for serving

Plain yogurt for serving

*makes 4 servings*

In a large sauté pan over medium-high heat, warm the oil. Add the onion and sauté until tender, about 5 minutes. Add the garlic and ginger and stir until fragrant, 1 minute. Add the cumin, coriander, and cayenne and stir until fragrant, 30 seconds.

Add the lamb, breaking up with a spatula. Sprinkle with 1½ teaspoons salt. Let the lamb cook for several minutes undisturbed, until it starts to develop a nice brown sear on the bottom. Stir and break up any larger pieces again. Cook until the lamb is browned and has some crispy edges, a few minutes longer. Reduce the heat to low and add the tomato paste and ⅓ cup (3 fl oz/80 ml) water, stirring to dissolve the tomato paste and scrape up any browned bits clinging to the bottom of the pan. Taste and adjust the seasoning, if necessary.

Heap the rice onto plates and spoon the lamb and peas on the side. Serve warm, passing the yogurt at the table.

# chapter 6: party food
## snacks, dinner, bbq & brunch

121   party tips

122   anytime party snacks

124   fresh dips & veggies

127   cheese plates

128   deviled eggs

128   pigs in blankets

129   parmesan & black pepper popcorn

129   salted caramel corn

130   cozy dinner party

133   home-style pot roast

134   creamy mashed potatoes

134   arugula salad with fennel & citrus

136   backyard barbeque

139   barbecue chicken with bourbon-molasses sauce

140   sweet corn with cream & chile

140   grilled garlic bread

142   lazy brunch

145   frittata remixes

146   monkey bread with pecans, bourbon & orange

147   bacon-wrapped sausages

"Entertaining" is something adults do when they invite people over and then proceed to freak out. Don't "entertain." Just have some friends over. It's way more fun. There is some effort involved: shopping, tidying, and stirring things at the last minute. But sharing a delicious meal with good friends is one of life's greatest pleasures, and it only gets easier with practice. Here are my top tips to get the party started.

# party tips

## buy more forks

How many friends are you inviting over? Do you own at least twice as many forks? Don't interrupt the conversation to do dishes between dinner and dessert. You'll never be sorry to own more forks.

## buy real wine glasses

They don't have to be expensive. They don't have to have stems. But it's nice if they're not red cups.

## keep it simple

Plan a menu that you can actually handle. If you're tackling a main course you haven't tried before, keep it easy with the sides. If you're making a couple of nibbles, round it out with something simple you can plunk onto plates, like cheese (see page 127), smoked fish, cured meats, olives, nuts, or veggies.

## make stuff ahead

Shop a day before the party. Prep dips, sauces, and desserts in advance. Stews and braises reheat beautifully.

## clean a little

Shove your stuff into closets, do the dishes, run a vacuum. But don't kill yourself. These are your friends! They know what you're like.

## don't mention cost

Don't ask friends to chip in on the bill, or allude to how expensive the fish was. If they offer to bring something, great! Or maybe they'll host next time.

## do accept help

You can't ask, but if they offer, go for it! Salad, wine, or dessert are all easy to delegate.

## make a plan of attack

Things that are awkward to be doing when guests arrive: vacuuming, cleaning the bathroom, applying mascara, blow drying your hair, wrestling with big dishes. Things that are charming to be doing when guests arrive: setting the table, opening wine, tossing salad. Big difference.

## never panic, never apologize

Julia Child said it best. Excuses are not going to make a bad dish any better, they'll just make your friends uncomfortable. You made a homemade meal! You're awesome! Relax and bon appétit.

# anytime
# party snacks

No matter the occasion—apartment warmings, birthdays, holidays—it's not a party without snacks. These are the nibbles to serve with drinks, easy to set out on a coffee table or pass around a crowd. The recipes are easy to scale if you're having a fabulous cocktail party of epic proportions. But quick dips, artisan cheeses, and other bites are delicious anytime, even for casual get-togethers.

From-scratch dips are an easy way to upgrade party fare. Feel free to mix and match dippers, from crunchy chips to colorful fresh veggies. Here are four dunk-worthy concoctions you can whip up in minutes.

# fresh dips & veggies

## guacamole

3 avocados, pitted and peeled

Juice of 1 lemon

$\frac{1}{2}$ teaspoon chile powder

Pinch of cayenne pepper

Salt

1 small tomato

$\frac{1}{4}$ cup ($\frac{1}{3}$ oz/10 g) chopped fresh cilantro leaves

Tortilla chips for serving

*makes about 2 cups (16 oz/500 g)*

*Guacamole is incredibly easy to smash and swirl, and inarguably better fresh. Press plastic wrap onto the surface to protect the pretty green color.*

In a bowl, add the avocados, lemon juice, chile, cayenne, and $\frac{1}{2}$ teaspoon salt and mash with a fork. Cut the tomato in half, and squeeze the halves gently, running a finger into the nooks and crannies to extract the seeds. Add the tomato and cilantro to the bowl with the avocado, and stir to combine. Taste and adjust the seasoning, if necessary. Serve the guacamole right away with tortilla chips on the side. Note: You can make up to a few hours ahead. Cover with plastic wrap, pressing directly onto the surface, and refrigerate until ready to serve.

## yogurt, cucumber & dill dip

$1\frac{1}{2}$ cups (12 oz/375 g) plain yogurt

$\frac{1}{2}$ cucumber, seeded and shredded or finely chopped

Grated zest and juice of $\frac{1}{2}$ lemon

$\frac{1}{4}$ cup ($\frac{1}{3}$ oz/10 g) fresh dill, minced

$\frac{1}{4}$ teaspoon onion powder

Salt and freshly ground pepper

Baby carrots, mini bell peppers, sugar snap peas, and cherry tomatoes for serving

Naan bread triangles for serving

*makes about 2 cups (16 oz/500 g)*

*Refreshing cucumber and yogurt are a lighter alternative to a cheese plate (page 127). Greek or regular yogurt works fine, just get unsweetened.*

In a bowl, add the yogurt, cucumber, lemon zest and juice, dill, onion powder, $\frac{1}{2}$ teaspoon salt, and a generous grind of pepper and stir to combine. Taste and adjust the seasoning. Cover and refrigerate for 1 hour to let the flavors blend. Serve the dip with veggies and naan bread.

# homemade hummus

1 can (15 oz/470 g) garbanzo beans, drained

2 tablespoons tahini paste

2 tablespoons olive oil, plus more for drizzling

Juice of ½ lemon

1 clove garlic, chopped

Salt

Sumac or smoked paprika for sprinkling

Dried oregano for sprinkling

Pita bread triangles for serving

*makes about 1½ cups (12 oz/375 g)*

*Hummus is extra fluffy and delicious when you do it yourself. Add a drizzle of olive oil and a sprinkle of sumac, the fragrant African spice.*

In a food processor or blender, add the garbanzo beans, tahini, olive oil, lemon juice, garlic, and 1 teaspoon salt and blend until thick and smooth. If you're using a blender, add 1 or 2 tablespoons of water if necessary to loosen. Scrape into a bowl. Drizzle with olive oil, sprinkle with sumac and oregano, and serve with pita bread on the side.

# romesco with roasted peppers

½ cup (2½ oz/75 g) blanched almonds, preferably Marcona

1 jar (12 oz/375 g) roasted red peppers in oil, drained

2 tablespoons extra-virgin olive oil

1 tablespoon red wine vinegar

1 clove garlic, chopped

1 teaspoon smoked paprika

Salt

Cooked shrimp for serving

Sliced baguette for serving

Grilled green onions, fennel, or asparagus for serving

*makes about 2 cups (16 oz/500 g)*

*Romesco is a rugged mix of vibrant red peppers, ground almonds, and smoky paprika. It's delicious with grilled meat, but also as a dip for prawns.*

In a food processor or blender, add almonds and pulse until finely chopped. Add the peppers, olive oil, vinegar, garlic, paprika, and 1 teaspoon salt and pulse until thick but still rough. Scrape into a bowl. Serve with prawns, baguette, and grilled green onions on the side.

... artisan cheeses and crusty breads are sure to impress.

*Sliced Cheddar and water crackers never hurt anyone, but artisan cheeses and crusty breads are sure to impress. Here are four ways to build a plate, with ideas for different cheese types and accompanying snacks and sips.*

# cheese plates

## spring

Fresh goat's milk (chevre, Crottin de Chavignol)

Herb-flavored semi-firm (Cotswold, dill Havarti)

Barnyardy washed-rind (Époisses, Reblochon, Taleggio)

Rainbow carrots

French radishes

Blanched asparagus

Sliced baguette

Grassy white wine (Sauvignon Blanc, Sancerre)

## summer

Fresh cow's milk (buffalo mozzarella, burrata)

Buttery semi-firm cow's milk (Mahón, fontina, Edam)

Aged sheep's milk (Manchego, pecorino)

Heirloom tomatoes

Sliced cucumber

Sliced bell pepper

Olive bread

Crisp white wine (Pinot Grigio, Prosecco, rosé)

Shopping Tip: When you're building a cheese plate, get a few different types, varying in texture and flavor. Flavor starts with milk: mellow and familiar cow's milk, tangy and grassy goat, briny and distinctive sheep. Texture is tied to aging: fresh and soft chevre, soft-ripened and gooey Brie, aged and semi-firm Gruyère, and so on. But you don't have to be a cheese snob to get something yummy tonight. Just learn the characteristics that you like, and when in doubt, ask the cheesemonger for a bite.

## fall

Crumbly clothbound cow's milk (Cheddar, Cheshire, Lancashire)

Bold blue cow's milk (Stilton, Roquefort, Valdeón)

Ash- or leaf-wrapped goat's milk (Sainte-Maure, Valençay, Humboldt Fog)

Sliced apples or pears

Halved figs

Honeycomb

Toasted walnuts

Multigrain bread

Fruit-forward red wine (Pinot Noir, Zinfandel)

Hoppy beer (IPA, brown ale) or dry cider

## winter

Soft-ripened and creamy (Brie, Brillat-Savarin, Explorateur)

Nutty semi-firm cow's milk (Comté, Emmentaler, Gouda)

Washed-rind and woodsy (Vacherin Mont d'Or, Försterkäse, Winnimere)

Medjool dates

Dried apricots

Pistachios

Toasted brioche

Dry sparkling wine (Brut Champagne)

Bold big-bodied red wine (Cabernet Sauvignon, Merlot)

*A good deviled egg is charming and old-fashioned without being fussy. This mustardy mix features vinegar, capers, and dill. Don't mess around with pastry bags. Just dollop, scatter with dill, and get back to the party.*

## deviled eggs

12 large eggs

¼ cup (2 fl oz/60 ml) mayo

¼ cup (2 oz/60 g) sour cream

1 tablespoon Dijon mustard

1 teaspoon Champagne vinegar

2 teaspoons capers, finely chopped

Salt and freshly ground pepper

Sweet paprika for sprinkling

Fresh dill sprigs for sprinkling

*makes 24 halves; about 12 servings*

Put the eggs in a saucepan and add enough cold water to cover by a couple of inches. Bring to a boil, remove from the heat, cover, and let rest for 20 minutes. Drain the eggs and rinse under cold water. When cool enough to handle, peel and halve the eggs.

Gently extract the yolks from the whites. In a bowl, add the yolks, mayo, sour cream, mustard, vinegar, capers, and ½ teaspoon salt and mash with a fork. Spoon the deviled mixture back into the egg white halves. Place the filled eggs on a large plate, cover, and refrigerate until ready to serve. The eggs can be made ahead and chilled for several hours.

When ready to serve, sprinkle the deviled eggs with paprika and dill and grind lightly with pepper.

*Guests never outgrow the delight of plump little sausages wrapped in pastry. No matter what other glamorous bites you're passing, the pigs will run out first. Double or triple this recipe, depending on the size of your invite list.*

## pigs in blankets

1 package (4 oz/125 g) crescent roll dough

Freshly ground pepper

16 mini sausages

Freshly grated Parmesan or shredded Cheddar for sprinkling

Grainy mustard for serving

Cornichons and pickled onions for serving

*makes 16 pigs; about 8 servings*

Preheat the oven to 350°F (180°C). Set out a large rimmed baking sheet.

On a work surface, unroll the dough. Separate and cut it into 16 triangles or rectangles. Grind with pepper. Take a piece of dough, place one sausage at the wider end, and snugly roll it up. Repeat with the remaining dough and sausages, spacing the rolled pigs on the prepared baking sheet. Sprinkle with Parmesan.

Bake until the sausages are plump and the pastry is golden brown, about 18 minutes. Let cool slightly, then transfer to a large plate. Serve warm with mustard and pickles on the side.

Prep Tip: Crank some tunes and recruit a friend or roommate to keep you company and help with rolling. You can cover and refrigerate the wrapped sausages for a few hours, and pop into the oven to bake right before the party.

*Skip the chips and go for freshly popped corn, a cheap and highly addictive bar snack. Sprinkle with freshly grated Parmesan and coarse black pepper for a savory edge.*

## parmesan & black pepper popcorn

1 tablespoon canola oil

1/2 cup (3 oz/90 g) popcorn kernels

1/4 cup (2 oz/60 g) unsalted butter, melted

1 cup (4 oz/125 g) freshly grated Parmesan cheese

Freshly ground black pepper

*makes about 12 cups (10 oz/315 g)*

In a deep sauté pan over medium-high heat, warm the oil. Add 3 of the kernels. When one pops, add the rest of the kernels, and cover tightly with the lid. Continue to cook, shaking the pan regularly to prevent from burning, until the popping subsides. When you can count for more than 3 seconds between pops, remove the pan from the heat and immediately pour all of the popcorn into a large bowl.

Drizzle the popcorn with the butter and toss to coat. Sprinkle with half of the Parmesan and a generous grind of pepper and toss to distribute throughout. Sprinkle with the remaining Parmesan, grind with pepper, and serve warm.

*Classic caramel corn involves boiling sugar to the brink of burning, which requires a candy thermometer, and it's risky business. This oven method takes away the stress, and the results are equally crunchy and delicious.*

## salted caramel corn

1 tablespoon canola oil

1/2 cup (3 oz/90 g) popcorn kernels

1/2 cup (4 oz/125 g) unsalted butter

1/2 cup (5 fl oz/160 ml) corn syrup or maple syrup

1/2 cup (3 1/2 oz/105 g) firmly packed brown sugar

1 teaspoon pure vanilla extract

1/2 teaspoon baking soda

1/2 teaspoon salt

Flaky sea salt, such as Maldon, for sprinkling

*makes about 12 cups (16 oz/500 g)*

Preheat the oven to 300°F (150°C). Line 2 large rimmed baking sheets with aluminum foil and spray with oil.

In a deep sauté pan over medium-high heat, warm the oil. Add 3 of the kernels. When one pops, add the rest of the kernels, and cover tightly with the lid. Continue to cook, shaking the pan regularly to prevent from burning, until the popping subsides. When you can count for more than 3 seconds between pops, remove the pan from the heat and immediately pour all of the popcorn into a large bowl.

In a saucepan over medium-high heat, melt the butter. Add the corn syrup and brown sugar and stir to combine. Bring to a simmer, reduce the heat, and simmer briskly, stirring regularly, until a thick syrup forms, 10 minutes. Watch to make sure it doesn't burn. Remove from the heat. Stir in the vanilla, baking soda, and 1/2 teaspoon salt. The mixture will turn frothy. Working quickly, pour over the popcorn, tossing to coat. Spread the coated popcorn onto the prepared pans.

Bake for 30 minutes, stirring twice, until the caramel is dark golden and crunchy. Let cool slightly, break into pieces, and cool completely. Pour into a large bowl, sprinkle with sea salt, and serve.

# cozy dinner party

Dinner parties don't have to be a big deal. This menu feeds 6 to 8, enough to gather a few good friends without overwhelming the conversation. I often serve roast chicken (page 79), salmon with lemony risotto (page 39), or prosciutto & arugula pizza (page 55). But pot roast is a reliable recommendation for aspiring hosts. It's surprisingly cheap, easy to make ahead, hard to mess up—and downright delicious.

Pot roast is a showstopper to haul out of the oven for a cozy dinner. When you lift the lid off the pot of glistening meat and hunks of root veggies, you'll catch a big whiff of wine and rosemary. Spoon lots of pan sauce over the mashed potatoes, add crunchy greens, and uncork a big bold red. I'm all about warm hazelnut brownies (page 152) or buttermilk chocolate cake (page 157) for dessert.

# home-style pot roast

3–4 lb (1.5–2 kg) chuck roast

Salt and freshly ground pepper

2 tablespoons olive oil

1 cup (8 fl oz/250 ml) dry red wine

1 cup (8 fl oz/250 ml) beef stock

1 tablespoon Worcestershire sauce

Sprig fresh thyme, or 1 teaspoon dried

Sprig fresh rosemary, or 1 teaspoon dried

1 dried bay leaf

3 cloves garlic, smashed but left whole

2 yellow onions, quartered

4 large carrots, cut into hunks

Mashed potatoes (page 134) for serving

makes 6 to 8 servings

Preheat the oven to 300°F (150°C). Sprinkle the chuck roast generously on all sides with salt and pepper. In a Dutch oven over medium-high heat, warm the olive oil. Add the roast and sear, turning, until browned all over, about 3 minutes per side. Transfer to a plate and set aside.

Return the pan to the stove and reduce the heat to low. Add the wine and stock, scraping up any browned bits clinging to the bottom of the pan. Add the Worcestershire, thyme, rosemary, and bay leaf and stir to combine. Return the roast to the pan, along with any juices that have accumulated on the plate. Scatter the garlic, onion, and carrots around the roast. Cover the pot tightly and transfer to the oven. Braise until the roast is fork tender, about 4 hours.

Transfer the pot roast to a cutting board and carve into thick slices. Heap mashed potatoes onto plates and place the sliced beef, onions, and carrots on the side. Spoon pan sauce over everything and serve warm.

Shopping Tip: As cuts of beef go, chuck is cheap and hard to mess up, as long as you leave enough time to braise it until tender. For less stress on party day, make it in advance; it reheats beautifully.

*Humble mashed potatoes are all about comfort. When you drain the potatoes, give them a minute or two to steam in the colander. The drier the spuds, the fluffier the mash. I sneak in a dollop of cheese, for extra creamy flavor.*

## creamy mashed potatoes

8 large russet potatoes (4 lb/2 kg), peeled and quartered

Salt

¼ cup (2 oz/60 g) unsalted butter

½ cup (4 oz/125 g) cream cheese

1 cup (8 fl oz/250 ml) milk

½ teaspoon onion powder

½ teaspoon ground white pepper

*makes 8 servings*

Put the potatoes in a pot, pour in cold water to cover, and salt generously. Bring to a boil and cook until tender when pierced with a fork, about 15 minutes. Drain and let steam in the colander for a minute or two. Return to the pot. Add the butter and cream cheese and press with a masher or wooden spoon to break up the potatoes. Once the butter and cheese have melted, add the milk, onion powder, white pepper, and 2 teaspoons salt and stir to combine. Taste and adjust the seasoning, if necessary. Serve warm.

*Balance a rich main with a super fresh salad, full of peppery arugula, anise-flavored fennel, and tart citrus. The citrus is flexible, if blood oranges prove hard to find. Meyer lemons are exceptionally sweet and fragrant.*

## arugula salad with fennel & citrus

for the dressing

1 tablespoon Dijon mustard

1 tablespoon red wine vinegar

Juice of ½ regular lemon

½ cup (4 fl oz/125 ml) extra-virgin olive oil

Salt and freshly ground pepper

1 grapefruit

1 blood or navel orange

1 Meyer lemon

1 fennel bulb

5 oz (155 g) arugula

*makes 8 servings*

To make the dressing, in a jar, combine the mustard, vinegar, lemon juice, olive oil, ½ teaspoon salt, and several grinds of pepper. Shake to combine. Taste and adjust the seasoning, if necessary.

To prepare the citrus, take the grapefruit, cut off the top and bottom, and stand it upright on the cutting board. Slicing down, cut off the peel and white pith, just grazing the juicy flesh, following the round shape of the fruit. Slice the flesh crosswise into rounds. Halve the rounds, if you like. Repeat with the orange and lemon. To prepare the fennel, remove and discard the stalks and fronds, reserving a few fronds for sprinkling, if you like. Trim the bottom. Slice the bulb in half lengthwise and remove the core. Place the cut sides down on the cutting board, and slice as thinly as possible across the grain.

In a large bowl, add the arugula, grapefruit, orange, lemon, and fennel bulb and toss to combine. Pour half of the dressing over and toss to coat. Taste a leaf and add more dressing as needed, and save any remaining for another use. Divide between plates, sprinkle with the fennel fronds, and serve.

I sneak in a dollop of cheese,
for extra creamy flavor.

# backyard barbecue

So your roommate owns a grill? It's time for some adventures in fire and smoke. This menu is big enough for a crew, with enough grub to feed a dozen rowdy friends. Sure, you could just do burgers and dogs. But sticky-sweet barbecue chicken, finger-lickin' baby back ribs, and sweet peaches are worth getting fired up about. Bust out a case of cold beer and start pouring mint juleps and cinnamon tea.

*Sticky-sweet barbecue sauce, dark with molasses and spiked with bourbon, is equally delicious over chicken or ribs. A bird and 3 racks should feed a dozen friends. Round out the menu with a pan of gooey mac and cheese (page 46), garlic bread, corn, and glazed peaches (page 163) for dessert.*

# barbecue chicken with bourbon-molasses sauce

for the bourbon-molasses sauce

2 cups (16 oz/500 g) ketchup

½ cup (5½ oz/170 g) molasses

½ cup (4 fl oz/125 ml) bourbon

¼ cup (2 oz/60 g) firmly packed brown sugar

1 tablespoon Worcestershire sauce

1 teaspoon chile powder

1 teaspoon garlic powder

1 teaspoon onion powder

Salt and freshly ground pepper

1 whole chicken, about 3 lb (1.5 kg), cut into 8 or 10 pieces

*makes 4 to 6 servings*

To make the barbecue sauce, in a small saucepan over medium-high heat, add the ketchup, molasses, bourbon, brown sugar, Worcestershire, chile powder, garlic powder, onion powder, and ½ teaspoon salt and whisk to combine. Bring to a simmer, reduce the heat to maintain, and simmer until the flavors have blended, about 10 minutes. Remove from the heat and let cool.

Place the chicken in a baking dish just large enough to hold it. Season generously with salt and pepper. Pour half of the cooled barbecue sauce over and turn to coat. Cover with plastic wrap, refrigerate, and marinate for at least 1 hour.

Pull the chicken out of the fridge to let it come to room temperature on the counter. Preheat the grill to medium heat. If you're working with charcoal, when the coals are gray at the edges, rake them across half of the bottom of the grill in a thick layer. Oil the grill rack.

Place the chicken over the hottest part of the grill and cook until well marked, turning once, about 8 minutes per side. Watch it carefully to make sure the barbecue sauce doesn't burn. Move the chicken to indirect heat, cover the grill, and continue to cook until firm and no longer pink at the center, 20 minutes longer.

Transfer the chicken to a platter and serve warm, with extra sauce on the side.

Grilling Tip: Sugary barbecue sauce burns easily. If you're using a charcoal grill, save a "cool zone" or "safety zone," as grill masters call it. Rake the coals over only part of the bottom of the grill, leaving a section empty. Then you can scoot the chicken over and cook it slowly, out of direct heat. Gas you can just turn down.

BBQ Hacks: Bourbon-Molasses Ribs

Preheat the oven to 350°F (180°C). Season **2 racks baby back ribs** (about 4 lb/ 2 kg) generously on both sides with **salt**, **pepper**, **chile powder**, and **cumin**. Place the racks in a large roasting pan or on a rimmed baking sheet and cover with foil. Bake until tender when pierced with a fork, about 1½ hours. Brush the ribs with **bourbon-molasses sauce** and grill, turning once or twice, until marked and glazed, about 10 minutes total. Transfer to a cutting board and let rest for a few minutes. Carve between the ribs to separate and serve warm, with extra sauce on the side.

*There are two ways to go with grilled corn. You can leave them in the husks, soak in saltwater, and steam. I prefer to shuck, brush with oil, and char directly on the grate. Go Latin street food style with lime, crema, and chile.*

## sweet corn with cream & chile

8 cobs sweet corn, shucked

Olive oil for brushing

Juice of 1 lime, plus wedges for serving

½ cup (4 oz/125 g) crema (see page 10) or sour cream

Ground chile powder for sprinkling

Salt

*makes 8 servings*

Preheat the grill to medium-high heat. If you're working with charcoal, when the coals are gray at the edges, rake them across the bottom in a thick layer.

Brush the corn with olive oil. Place the corn over the hottest part of the grill in a single layer. Cover the grill and cook, turning once or twice, until the corn is marked and tender, about 10 minutes total.

Transfer the corn to a platter. Squeeze the lime juice over. Drizzle with the crema, sprinkle with chile and salt, and serve warm.

*Hang onto your tongs and stand by while grilling bread—it's a quick toast over the coals, only a minute or two per side. The brave are rewarded with gorgeous grill marks, melted garlic butter, and big smoky flavor.*

## grilled garlic bread

½ cup (4 oz/125 g) unsalted butter

4 cloves garlic, minced or mashed to a paste

Salt

1 loaf ciabatta or country-style bread, split

Smoked paprika for sprinkling

Chopped fresh flat-leaf parsley for sprinkling

*makes 8 servings*

Preheat the grill to medium-high heat. If you're working with charcoal, when the coals are gray at the edges, rake them across the bottom in a thick layer.

In a saucepan over medium heat, melt the butter. Add the garlic and a pinch of salt and stir until fragrant, 3 minutes. Using a pastry brush, generously brush the garlic butter onto the cut sides of the ciabatta.

Place the ciabatta on the grill and toast, turning once, until marked, about 3 minutes total, working quickly and watching the bread carefully to make sure it doesn't burn. Transfer to a cutting board and let cool slightly.

Cut the garlic bread into thick slices, sprinkle with smoked paprika and parsley, and serve warm.

# lazy brunch

Brunch! The ultimate competitive sport for young urban foodies. Skip the waitlist and lines, and do it yourself. Whether you're recovering from a hangover or looking for another excuse for day drinking, Sunday morning always shines a little bit brighter with the prospect of savory eggs, sweet bread, and bacon-wrapped sausages.

Frittatas are pretty, rustic, and dead easy. Cooked and served in one pan, you can take the same skillet from stovetop to oven to table. A reliable cast-iron skillet is the way to go, but an ovenproof frying pan will work in a pinch. Feel free to customize with whatever mix-ins—meat, veggies, or cheese—you have on hand.

# frittata remixes

*each recipe makes 6 servings*

## ham, leeks & gruyere

12 large eggs

Salt and freshly ground pepper

1 tablespoon olive oil

1 leek, white and pale green parts only, chopped

8 oz (250 g) chopped ham

1 cup (4 oz/125 g) shredded Gruyère cheese

Chopped chives for sprinkling

Preheat the oven to 450°F (230°C). In a large bowl, whisk the eggs, ½ teaspoon salt, and a grind of pepper. In a large cast-iron skillet over medium-high heat, warm the oil. Add the leek and sauté until tender, 5 minutes. Add the ham and stir to warm through, 3 minutes. Pour the eggs over, sprinkle with the Gruyère, and cook just until the edges start to brown, 3 minutes. Transfer the pan to the oven and bake until puffed and golden, about 10 minutes longer. Sprinkle with chives, slice into thick wedges, and serve warm.

## zucchini, red pepper & oregano

12 large eggs

Salt and freshly ground pepper

1 tablespoon olive oil

1 small zucchini, thinly sliced

1 red bell pepper, seeded and thinly sliced

1 clove garlic, minced

1 cup (4 oz/125 g) shredded mozzarella

Chopped fresh oregano leaves for sprinkling

Preheat the oven to 450°F (230°C). In a large bowl, whisk the eggs, ½ teaspoon salt, and a grind of pepper. In a large cast-iron skillet over medium-high heat, warm the oil. Add the zucchini and pepper, sprinkle with salt, and sauté until tender, 5 minutes. Add the garlic and stir until fragrant, 1 minute. Pour the eggs over, sprinkle with the mozzarella, and cook just until the edges start to brown, 3 minutes. Transfer the pan to the oven and bake until puffed and golden, 10 minutes longer. Sprinkle with oregano, slice into thick wedges, and serve warm.

## broccoli, bacon & cheddar

12 large eggs

Salt and freshly ground pepper

3 thick slices bacon

1 tablespoon olive oil

1 cup (4 oz/125 g) chopped broccoli

1 clove garlic, minced

1 cup (4 oz/125 g) shredded sharp Cheddar cheese

Preheat the oven to 450°F (230°C). In a large bowl, whisk the eggs, ½ teaspoon salt, and a grind of pepper. Warm a large cast-iron skillet over medium-high heat. Add the bacon and cook, turning once, until crisp and brown, 10 minutes total. Transfer to a paper-towel lined plate, and when cool, crumble. Wipe out the pan, return to medium-high heat, and warm the oil. Add the broccoli and sauté until tender, 5 minutes. Add the garlic and stir until fragrant, 1 minute. Add the crumbled bacon. Pour the eggs over, sprinkle with the Cheddar, and cook just until the edges start to brown, 3 minutes. Transfer the pan to the oven and bake until puffed and golden, 10 minutes longer. Grind with pepper, slice into thick wedges, and serve warm.

## potato, onion & manchego

12 large eggs

Salt and freshly ground pepper

1 tablespoon olive oil

1 large Yukon gold potato, thinly sliced

½ yellow onion, thinly sliced

1 cup (4 oz/125 g) shredded Manchego cheese

Smoked paprika for sprinkling

Preheat the oven to 450°F (230°C). In a large bowl, whisk the eggs, ½ teaspoon salt, and a grind of pepper. In a large cast-iron skillet over medium-high heat, warm the oil. Add the potato and onion, sprinkle with salt, and sauté until the potatoes are tender, 10 minutes. Pour the eggs over, sprinkle with the Manchego, and cook just until the edges start to brown, 3 minutes. Transfer the pan to the oven and bake until puffed and golden, 10 minutes longer. Sprinkle with paprika, slice into thick wedges, and serve warm.

You don't have to be a baking pro to satisfy a morning sweet tooth. Monkey bread is super simple and fun to pick apart with friends. Roll pinches of biscuit dough in a bath of butter, brown sugar, and cinnamon, and fold in pecans, bourbon, and orange zest to push it over the top.

# monkey bread with pecans, bourbon & orange

2 packages (16 oz/500 g *each*) biscuit dough

½ cup (4 oz/125 g) unsalted butter

1 cup (7 oz/220 g) firmly packed brown sugar

1 teaspoon ground cinnamon

¼ cup (2 fl oz/60 ml) bourbon

1 teaspoon pure vanilla extract

½ cup (2 oz/60 g) pecans, toasted (see note on page 151) and chopped

Grated zest of 1 orange

Pinch of salt

Flaky sea salt, such as Maldon, for sprinkling

*makes 8 servings*

Preheat the oven to 350°F (180°C). Butter a Bundt pan. Separate the dough and pinch or cut into bite-size pieces. Transfer to a large bowl and set aside.

In a small sauté pan over medium heat, melt the butter. Add the brown sugar, cinnamon, bourbon, and vanilla and stir until the sugar has completely dissolved, about 5 minutes. Remove from the heat and stir in the pecans, orange zest, and pinch of salt. Pour the butter mixture over the pieces of dough in the bowl, and turn to coat. Scrape the dough mixture into the prepared Bundt pan.

Bake until the pastry is puffed and the surface is golden brown, about 30 minutes. Let cool slightly, then turn the monkey bread out onto a serving plate. Sprinkle lightly with salt and serve warm, letting guests pick apart the hunks of bread at the table.

*Pig wrapped in pig is an outrageous treat. My boyfriend's family introduced me to this delicacy, which they serve at special-occasion dinners. My family loves them with sticky buns in the morning. I am here to tell you—stabbing a bacon-wrapped sausage with a fork while still wearing pajamas is a deeply satisfying experience.*

# bacon-wrapped sausages

**12 thin slices bacon**

**12 pork breakfast sausages**

*makes 6 servings*

Preheat the oven to 450°F (230°C). Line a rimmed baking sheet with foil.

On a cutting board, take a slice of bacon, place a sausage at one end, and snugly roll it up. You'll want to use a slight angle, and overlap the bacon by about a third, to help it stay together. If the bacon is too long, trim the end with a paring knife. (Save the trimmings for another use, like jacket potatoes, page 27, or broccoli frittata, page 145.) Repeat with the remaining bacon and sausages, spacing the rolled sausages on the prepared baking sheet.

Bake until the bottoms start to brown, 12 minutes. Remove the pan from the oven, taking care not to spill or spatter hot fat. If necessary, spoon or pour any excess fat into a bowl. (When cool, discard or reserve for another use.) Use tongs to flip the sausages. Return to the oven and bake until crisp and browned, 10 minutes longer.

Transfer to a platter, let cool slightly, and serve.

Shopping Tip: Make sure to buy thinly sliced bacon (or at least not thick cut), which wraps around the sausages the best. The sausages plump, the bacon crisps into a tender embrace. It's a beautiful friendship on your brunch plate.

# chapter 7: guilty pleasures
## sweets & snacks

151   killer chocolate chip cookies

152   one-bowl brownies with hazelnuts & nutella

154   marshmallow crispy treats with vanilla bean

155   monster granola bars

157   chocolate cake with mocha buttercream

158   confetti cupcakes

160   carrot cake with cream cheese frosting

161   cinnamon-apple crumble

163   grilled peaches with mascarpone & almonds

164   greek yogurt with mango & honey

164   whipped ricotta with berries

166   chunky monkey banana bread

167   spiced pumpkin bread

169   magical ginger chai

169   perfect hot cocoa

*I've been studying the art of the chocolate chip cookie since age 6. Over the years, I've discovered two things. First, cream the bejesus out of the butter and sugar, but take it easy on the dry ingredients. Second, chill the dough for 24–48 hours. I know. I'm sorry! As a reward for your patience, something magical happens to the gluten in the flour and the cookies emerge from the oven golden on the outside, gooey inside.*

# killer chocolate chip cookies

1 cup (8 oz/250 g)
unsalted butter, chilled

1 cup (7 oz/220 g) firmly
packed golden brown sugar

1/2 cup (4 oz/125 g)
granulated sugar

2 large eggs

2 tablespoons maple syrup

2 teaspoons pure vanilla extract

2 1/2 cups (12 1/2 oz/390 g)
all-purpose flour

1 teaspoon baking soda

1/2 teaspoon salt

1 cup (4 oz/125 g) walnuts,
toasted (see note) and finely
chopped

1 cup (6 oz/185 g)
chocolate chips

*makes 2 1/2 dozen cookies*

In the bowl of a stand mixer fitted with the paddle attachment, add the butter, brown sugar, and granulated sugar and beat on medium-high speed until fluffy. (If you don't have a stand mixer, start with room temperature butter in a large mixing bowl, and stir aggressively with a wooden spoon.) Add the eggs and beat to combine. Add the maple syrup and vanilla extract and beat to combine.

In a bowl, add the flour, baking soda, and salt and whisk to combine. Add the dry ingredients to the butter mixture and beat on low speed just until the dough comes together, a few strokes. Fold in the walnuts and chocolate chips. Cover with plastic wrap, pressing the plastic directly onto the surface of the dough. Chill for 24–48 hours.

Preheat the oven to 375°F (190°C). Drop heaping tablespoons of dough onto baking sheets, spacing them a few inches apart. Bake until the cookies turn golden at the edges but are still dense at the center, 8–10 minutes. Let rest for a few minutes on the pan.

Serve the cookies while gooey and warm. Let any remaining cookies cool completely on the pans, transfer to an airtight container, and store for a few days.

Prep Tip: We all take shortcuts in the kitchen, but I always take the time to toast nuts. It maximizes the flavor. Spread the walnuts on a baking sheet and toast in a 350°F (180°C) oven for about 10 minutes, stirring a couple of times. You can also use a dry pan over medium-high heat or a toaster oven, but keep an eye on them, so they don't burn! Either way, they're done when they're fragrant. Pour onto a cutting board, chop, and set aside to cool.

*A perfectly dense, fudgy brownie is a beautiful thing. But if you dare to embellish, here's a seductive addition. Fold a handful of roasted hazelnuts into the batter, and pour the world's most addictive chocolate spread on top after baking. If you're hosting a dinner party, pull a warm pan of hazelnut brownies out of the oven, and set a carton of vanilla ice cream on the table. It never fails to make friends swoon.*

# one-bowl brownies with hazelnuts & nutella

½ cup (4 oz/125 g) unsalted butter, melted and cooled

1 cup (8 oz/250 g) sugar

2 large eggs

1 teaspoon pure vanilla extract

⅔ cup (3½ oz/105 g) all-purpose flour

⅓ cup (1 oz/30 g) unsweetened cocoa powder

½ teaspoon salt

½ cup (2½ oz/75 g) hazelnuts, toasted (see note on page 151) and roughly chopped

½ cup (5 oz/155 g) chocolate-hazelnut spread, such as Nutella

*makes 16 squares*

Preheat the oven to 300°F (150°C). Butter an 8-by-8-inch (20-by-20-cm) baking pan.

In a large mixing bowl, add the butter and sugar and whisk to combine. Add the eggs and beat until thick and smooth. Add the vanilla and stir to combine. Add the flour, cocoa, and salt and stir gently just until the batter comes together, a few strokes. Fold in the hazelnuts.

Scrape the batter into the prepared pan, spreading evenly and smoothing the top. Bake until the brownies look set but a toothpick inserted at the center still comes away with a few moist crumbs, 40 minutes. Let cool slightly.

Scrape the chocolate-hazelnut spread into a small bowl and microwave until warm and loose, 30 seconds. Pour over the brownies, spreading evenly. Let rest for a few minutes until set.

Cut the brownies into squares and serve. Let any remaining brownies cool completely, cover the pan tightly, and store for a few days.

Prep Tip: Ingredients like salt and vanilla require a steady hand if you're measuring directly over the bowl—and there's not much you can do if you mess up. Save yourself the anxiety, and set a small bowl on the side. When you hit the right amount, add it to the main recipe.

My friend Kate is a crispy treat fanatic, and she's in good company these days. The masses have taken to social media, melting and mixing variations of the American classic. Get creative with your favorite sugary cereal from childhood, or go crazy with cookies, candy, and sweet sauces. Kate is into sprinkles, I'm all about peanut butter and chocolate, but no matter your guilty pleasure, there's a way to hack a crispy treat.

# marshmallow crispy treats with vanilla bean

¼ cup (2 oz/60 g) unsalted butter

1 vanilla bean or ½ teaspoon pure vanilla extract

Pinch of salt

1 bag (10 oz/315 g) mini marshmallows

4 cups (5 oz/155 g) puffed rice cereal

*makes 16 squares*

Lightly butter an 8-by-8 inch (20-by-20-cm) baking pan and a silicon spatula.

In a large pot over medium heat, melt the butter. Using a paring knife, slit the vanilla bean lengthwise. Use the tip of the knife to open the pod and expose the seeds. Scrape the seeds into a small pile. Add the vanilla seeds (or extract) and salt to the melted butter, and stir until fragrant, 1 minute.

Add the marshmallows and stir until melted, about 5 minutes. Remove from the heat. Add the cereal and stir to combine. Working quickly and using the buttered spatula, scrape the mixture into the prepared pan, pressing evenly to smooth the top. Let cool until set, 1 hour.

Cut the crispy treats into squares and serve. For any remaining crispy treats, cover the pan tightly, and store for a few days.

Crispy Treat Hacks

Captain's Crispy Treats: Replace the rice cereal with **Captain Crunch**.

Cocoa Crispy Treats: Replace the rice cereal with **Cocoa Pebbles**.

Cookies & Cream Crispy Treats: Add **8 crumbled Oreos** to the warm mixture.

Cake Batter Crispy Treats: Double **the vanilla** and add ¼ cup (1½ oz/45 g) **multicolored sprinkles** to the warm mixture.

M&M Crispy Treats: Press ½ cup (3 oz/90 g) **mini M&M's** on top before cooling.

Peanut Butter & Chocolate Crispy Treats: Add ¼ cup (2½ oz/75 g) **peanut butter** to the warm mixture. Spread **1 cup (6 oz/185 g) chocolate chips**, melted, on the surface. Sprinkle with **4 chopped chocolate peanut butter cups** before cooling.

Salted Caramel Crispy Treats: Add ½ cup (4 fl oz/185 ml) **caramel sauce** to the warm mixture. Sprinkle with **flaky sea salt** before serving.

Butter Pecan Crispy Treats: Add ½ cup (3½ oz/105 g) firmly packed **brown sugar** to the melting butter. Add ½ cup (2 oz/60 g) **chopped toasted pecans** (see note on page 151) to the warm mixture. Sprinkle with **flaky sea salt** before serving.

*Is there a more satisfying snack combo in this world than chocolate, nuts, and coconut? The hardest part about making these is that I have to resist the urge to devour the whole pan. I like my granola bars on the chewy side, so I bake them a scant 20 minutes, until the edges are just turning toasty. If you prefer crunchy, bake until deeply golden, a few minutes longer. Keep in mind that the bars will continue to crisp as they cool.*

# monster granola bars

2 cups (6 oz/185 g) rolled oats

1/2 cup (1/2 oz/15 g) puffed rice cereal

1/2 cup (2 oz/60 g) sliced almonds

1/2 cup (1 1/2 oz/45 g) unsweetened coconut flakes

1/2 cup (6 oz/185 g) honey

1/2 cup (5 oz/155 g) almond or peanut butter

1/4 cup (2 oz/60 g) firmly packed brown sugar

2 tablespoons olive oil

1 teaspoon pure vanilla extract

1/4 teaspoon salt

1/4 cup (1 1/2 oz/45 g) mini chocolate chips

*makes about 16 bars*

Preheat the oven to 350°F (180°C). Oil a 9-by-13-inch (23-by-33-cm) baking pan.

In a large bowl, add the oats, rice cereal, almonds, and coconut and stir to combine. In a small saucepan over medium heat, add the honey, almond butter, brown sugar, olive oil, vanilla, and salt. Stir until warm and loose, 5 minutes. Pour over the oats and stir to coat.

Scrape the mixture into the prepared pan, sprinkle with the chocolate chips, and press evenly to smooth the top. Bake until the oats are toasty and golden at the edges, about 20 minutes. Let cool slightly, slice into bars, and then let cool completely in the pan.

Serve the granola bars. For any remaining granola bars, cover the pan tightly, and store for a few days.

*This cake is a Duffett family classic. Tender buttermilk cake is stacked with a thick mocha frosting, with a hint of coffee, but a whole lot of vanilla. Assembling the layers looks harder than it is. Just butter the pans well, and smooth the frosting over the crumbs. Even wonky results taste delicious.*

# chocolate cake with mocha buttercream

4 oz (125 g) unsweetened chocolate, coarsely chopped

1 cup (8 oz/250 g) unsalted butter

4 large eggs

1 cup (8 fl oz/250 ml) buttermilk

2 cups (1 lb/500 g) granulated sugar

2 teaspoons pure vanilla extract

2 cups (10 oz/315 g) all-purpose flour

1½ teaspoons baking soda

½ teaspoon salt

for the frosting

1 cup (8 oz/250 g) unsalted butter, at room temperature

4 cups (1 lb/500 g) confectioners' sugar

¼ cup (¾ oz/20 g) unsweetened cocoa powder

¼ teaspoon salt

¼ cup (2 fl oz/60 ml) strong coffee, cooled

1 teaspoon pure vanilla extract

*makes 12 servings*

Preheat the oven to 350°F (180°C). Butter two 9-inch (23-cm) round cake pans. Line the bottom of the pans with rounds of parchment paper and butter the paper. Dust with flour and tap out any excess.

In a heatproof bowl set over (but not touching) simmering water, add the chocolate and butter and stir until melted, glossy, and smooth. Remove from the heat and let cool. (Alternatively, you can microwave in a glass measuring cup until melted, stopping and stirring every minute to make sure the chocolate doesn't burn.)

In a large mixing bowl, add the eggs and whisk until frothy. Add the buttermilk, granulated sugar, and vanilla. In another bowl, add the flour, baking soda, and salt and whisk to combine. Add the dry ingredients to the wet ingredients, and stir just until a few streaks remain. Add the melted chocolate and stir just until combined.

Divide the batter between the prepared pans, spreading evenly and smoothing the tops. Bake until a toothpick inserted at the center of a cake comes out clean, 25–30 minutes. Let cool completely in the pans, several hours.

To make the frosting, in the bowl of a stand mixer, beat the butter. (If you don't own a stand mixer, you can use a large mixing bowl with an electric handheld mixer.) Add 1 cup (4 oz/125 g) of the confectioners' sugar, the cocoa, salt, and coffee and beat on low speed to combine. Gradually beat in the remaining confectioners' sugar, raise the speed to high, and continue to beat until light and fluffy. Stir in the vanilla last.

When the cakes are completely cool, run a knife around the inside of a pan to loosen the sides. Place a serving plate on top, invert the pan, and gently ease the layer out. Peel off the parchment. Spread with a third of the frosting. Repeat with the second layer, stacking on top of the first. Frost the top and sides of the cake, working in the same direction to help smooth and seal in any crumbs. (If the crumbs give you a hard time, start with what's called a crumb coat, spreading a very thin layer of frosting over the top and sides. Refrigerate for 30 minutes to set, then spread with the remaining frosting.) Refrigerate until ready to serve.

Slice the cake into thick wedges and serve.

*I remember rainbow cakes made from mixes at dorm birthdays. Ditch the boxes and make these yourself. Confetti cupcakes are really just a basic white cake with sprinkles mixed in. You can totally handle that, and you can't beat homemade cake batter. Look for long, waxy sprinkles, sometimes called jimmies, rather than short, round sprinkles. Jimmies melt the best, creating those bursts of color in the interior of each pretty little cake.*

# confetti cupcakes

½ cup (4 oz/125 g) unsalted butter, chilled

1 cup (8 oz/250 g) granulated sugar

**4 large egg whites (see note)**

**1 teaspoon pure vanilla extract**

**2 cups (8 oz/250 g) cake or all-purpose flour**

**1 tablespoon baking powder**

¼ teaspoon salt

½ cup (4 fl oz/125 ml) milk

¼ cup (1½ oz/45 g) multicolored jimmies (see note), plus more for decorating

for the frosting

½ cup (4 oz/125 g) unsalted butter, at room temperature

3 cups (12 oz/375 g) confectioners' sugar

¼ cup (2 fl oz/60 ml) whole milk

**Pinch of salt**

½ teaspoon pure vanilla extract

*makes 12 cupcakes*

Preheat the oven to 325°F (165°C). Line a standard 12-cup muffin pan with paper liners or butter and dust with flour and tap out any excess.

In the bowl of a stand mixer fitted with the paddle attachment, add the butter and granulated sugar and beat on medium-high speed until fluffy. (If you don't have a stand mixer, start with room temperature butter in a large mixing bowl, and stir aggressively with a wooden spoon.) Add the egg whites and beat to combine. Stir in the vanilla.

In a separate bowl, add the flour, baking powder, and salt and whisk to combine. Add the dry ingredients to the wet ingredients, and beat on low speed just until a few streaks remain. Add the milk and beat just until combined, a few strokes. Fold in the jimmies.

Divide the batter between the prepared muffin cups, filling them about three-fourths full. Bake until a toothpick inserted at the center of a cupcake comes out clean, 20–25 minutes. Let cool slightly in the pan, transfer to a wire rack, and let cool completely.

To make the frosting, in the bowl of a stand mixer, beat the butter. (If you don't own a stand mixer, you can use a large mixing bowl with an electric handheld mixer.) Add 1 cup (4 oz/125 g) of the confectioners' sugar, the milk, and salt and beat on low speed to combine. Gradually beat in the remaining confectioners' sugar, raise the speed to high, and continue to beat until light and fluffy. Stir in the vanilla last.

When the cupcakes are completely cool, spread with the frosting. Decorate with additional sprinkles, if you like, and serve.

Prep Tip: Separating eggs scares some people. Take a deep breath. If you get a wisp of yolk into this batter—or even give up and use whole eggs—your cupcakes will still be delicious. They'll just be yellow cake, not white cake. To separate the eggs, set out two bowls. Crack an egg in half. Working over the first bowl, gently swap the yolk between the shell halves, letting the white slip through. Plop the yolk into the second bowl, and repeat with the remaining eggs.

My aunt Sally makes legendary carrot cake. Her recipe is super simple, but it's worth noting that she lives in Taos, and relies on real Mexican vanilla and local pecans. Quality ingredients make the cake! I used her basic formula, with a few tweaks. Most carrot cakes call for oil, but I'm all about butter. I added orange zest, spices, and raisins. And I slathered cream cheese frosting laced with bourbon on top. It just felt like the right thing to do.

## carrot cake with cream cheese frosting

1 cup (8 oz/250 g) unsalted butter, melted and cooled

2 cups (1 lb/500 g) granulated sugar

4 large eggs

2 teaspoons pure vanilla extract

Grated zest of 1 orange

2 cups (10 oz/315 g) all-purpose flour

2 teaspoons ground cinnamon

1 teaspoon ground ginger

$1/4$ teaspoon ground nutmeg

2 teaspoons baking soda

$1/2$ teaspoon salt

3 cups (15 oz/470 g) shredded carrots

1 cup (4 oz/125 g) chopped pecans, toasted (see note on page 151)

1 cup (6 oz/185 g) raisins

for the cream-cheese frosting

$1/4$ cup (2 oz/60 g) unsalted butter, at room temperature

8 oz (250 g) cream cheese, at room temperature

$1 1/2$ cups (6 oz/185 g) confectioners' sugar

Pinch of salt

1 tablespoon bourbon

makes 12 servings

Preheat the oven to 350°F (180°C). Butter a 9-by-13-inch (23-by-33-inch) baking pan.

In a large mixing bowl, add the butter, granulated sugar, and eggs and whisk to combine. Stir in the vanilla and orange zest. In a separate bowl, add the flour, cinnamon, ginger, nutmeg, baking soda, and salt and stir to combine. Add the dry ingredients to the wet ingredients and stir just until combined, a few strokes. Fold in the carrots, pecans, and raisins.

Scrape the batter into the prepared pan, spreading evenly and smoothing the top. Bake until a toothpick inserted at the center comes out clean, 35–40 minutes. Let cool completely in the pan.

To make the frosting, in the bowl of a stand mixer, beat the butter and cream cheese. (If you don't own a stand mixer, you can use a large mixing bowl with an electric handheld mixer.) Add the confectioners' sugar and salt and beat on low speed to combine. Raise the speed to high and continue to beat until light and fluffy. Stir in the bourbon last.

When the cake is completely cool, spread with the frosting. Cut the cake into squares and serve.

Tools Tip: A food processor with the shredding attachment will make short work of the carrots. But if you don't own one, a tried-and-true box grater-shredder gets the job done.

This autumn dessert is even easier than the proverbial pie. Chop up a few apples, sprinkle with a brown sugar topping, and pop the pan into the oven. The scent of cinnamon will quickly fill the kitchen. Top steaming bowls with a dollop of Greek yogurt, which is exceptionally thick and creamy, or a scoop of old-fashioned vanilla ice cream.

# cinnamon-apple crumble

for the topping

1/2 cup (4 oz/125 g) unsalted butter, at room temperature

1/2 cup (3 1/2 oz/105 g) firmly packed brown sugar

1/2 cup (2 1/2 oz/75 g) all-purpose flour

1 cup (3 oz/90 g) rolled oats

1/2 teaspoon ground cinnamon

Pinch of ground nutmeg

Pinch of salt

4 tart green apples, such as Granny Smith

Juice of 1 lemon

1 tablespoon all-purpose flour

1/2 teaspoon ground cinnamon

Greek yogurt for dolloping

makes 4 to 6 servings

Preheat the oven to 350°F (180°C). Butter an 8-by-8-inch (20-by-20-cm) baking pan.

To make the topping, in a bowl, add the butter and brown sugar and beat with a wooden spoon until fluffy. Add the flour, oats, cinnamon, nutmeg, and salt, and stir to combine. Set aside.

Core and chop the apples into bite-size pieces, adding them to a bowl as you work, and squeezing the lemon over and tossing to keep the apples from browning. Sprinkle the flour and cinnamon over the apples and toss to coat.

Pour the apples into the prepared pan. Sprinkle with the topping. Bake until the apples are tender and the topping is golden and bubbling, 30 minutes. Spoon the crumble into bowls, dollop with Greek yogurt, and serve warm.

Serving Tip: If you like, you can make these as individual servings. Butter large ramekins, soufflé dishes, or mugs—just make sure they're ovenproof. Place them on a large rimmed baking sheet before sliding them into the oven.

This summer treat is a sticky-sweet finale for a backyard barbecue (page 136). Luscious stone fruit, brushed with olive oil and maple, caramelizes gorgeously on the grill, melding into a dynamic combination of sweet, savory, and smoky flavors. Dollop some creamy mascarpone, the sweet dessert cheese, into the center of each peach. You won't be able to resist licking the spoon.

## grilled peaches with mascarpone & almonds

4 peaches, halved and pitted

Olive oil for brushing

Maple syrup or honey for brushing

1/2 cup (4 oz/125 g) mascarpone cheese

1/4 cup (1 oz/30 g) sliced almonds, toasted (see note on page 151)

*makes 4 servings*

Preheat the grill or a grill pan over medium-high heat. If you're working with charcoal, when the coals are gray at the edges, rake them across the bottom of the grill in a thick layer.

Brush the cut side of the peaches with olive oil. Place the peaches, cut side down, on the grill and cook until marked, about 3 minutes. Turn and brush with maple syrup. Cook for a couple of minutes longer, until the syrup glazes the fruit.

Place the grilled peaches on plates. Divide the mascarpone among the halves, spooning a dollop into the center of each cavity. Sprinkle with the almonds and serve warm.

*Thick, tangy Greek yogurt is equally tempting for breakfast or dessert. Don't worry about measuring exactly, just dollop and drizzle as you like. Pile on any variety of fresh, seasonal fruit. I'm partial to sweet-tart mango.*

## greek yogurt with mango & honey

2 cups (16 oz/500 g) plain Greek yogurt

2 cups (10 oz/315 g) chopped fresh fruit, such as mango

Honey for drizzling

Ground cinnamon for sprinkling

*makes 4 servings*

Spoon the yogurt into bowls and pile the fruit on top. Drizzle with honey, sprinkle with cinnamon, and serve.

*This is one of my favorite fresh, healthy desserts for busy weeknights. Fluffy ricotta cheese, lightly sweetened, makes a tempting base for juicy summer berries. Use part-skim ricotta to keep the calorie count low.*

## whipped ricotta with berries

2 cups (8 oz/250 g) mixed berries, such as strawberries, raspberries, and blackberries

Juice of 1/2 lemon

1 tablespoon granulated sugar

8 oz (250 g) fresh ricotta cheese

1/4 cup (1 oz/30 g) confectioners' sugar

1/2 teaspoon pure vanilla extract

Pinch of salt

Chopped fresh mint leaves for sprinkling

*makes 4 servings*

Hull and halve or quarter the strawberries, depending on their size. Place all of the berries in a bowl. Drizzle with the lemon juice, sprinkle with the granulated sugar, and turn to coat. Let the berries rest and release their juices, about 30 minutes.

In a separate bowl, add the ricotta, confectioners' sugar, vanilla, and salt. Whisk until light and fluffy.

Spoon the whipped ricotta into bowls and pile the berries on top. Sprinkle with mint and serve.

My friend and photographer Matt told me that we should have a banana bread in the cookbook. I always like Matt's ideas, and he's right—every young cook needs this reliable recipe. Who doesn't end up with a few bananas languishing into freckled sweetness? Who doesn't love banana bread, with or without nuts, with or without chocolate? Bake this on a lazy weekend, and grab a slice when you're running out the door to work.

# chunky monkey banana bread

½ cup (4 oz/125 g) unsalted butter, melted and cooled

1 cup (7 oz/220 g) firmly packed brown sugar

2 large eggs

3 really ripe bananas, mashed

1 teaspoon pure vanilla extract

1½ cups (7½ oz/235 g) all-purpose flour

1 teaspoon baking soda

1 teaspoon baking powder

½ teaspoon salt

1 teaspoon ground cinnamon

¼ teaspoon ground cloves

¼ teaspoon ground nutmeg

½ cup (2 oz/60 g) walnuts, toasted (see note on page 151) and roughly chopped

½ cup (3 oz/90 g) chocolate chips

*makes 9 servings*

Preheat the oven to 350°F (180°C). Butter a 5-by-9-inch (13-by-23-cm) loaf pan.

In a large mixing bowl, add the butter and brown sugar and whisk to combine. Add the eggs and beat until thick and smooth. Add the mashed bananas and vanilla and stir to combine.

In a separate bowl, add the flour, baking soda, baking powder, salt, cinnamon, cloves, and nutmeg and whisk with a fork to combine. Add the dry ingredients to the wet ingredients and stir just until combined, a few strokes. Fold in the walnuts and chocolate chips.

Scrape the batter into the prepared pan, spreading evenly and smoothing the top. Bake until a toothpick inserted at the center comes out clean or with only a few moist crumbs attached, 45–50 minutes. (If you hit a melted chocolate chip, it won't really be "clean," but you know what I mean.) Let cool in the pan.

Run a knife around the inside of the pan to loosen the sides. Placing one hand on top of the bread, invert the pan and gently ease the bread out onto a board or plate. Slice the banana bread thickly and serve.

Housekeeping Tip: Whenever your bananas start to go squidgy, chuck them into the freezer. You can pull them out on the weekend, when you actually have time for baking projects. Zap for a minute or so in the microwave. They do go black, but no need for alarm. I peel mine over the sink, arms outstretched, squinting slightly, muttering, "Ick, ick, ick!" But the old adage is reliably true: The browner the banana, the sweeter the bread.

*I once wrote an annoyed blog post about the demise of Starbucks' pumpkin bread. In retaliation, I developed a recipe that's even better: pure pumpkin, packed with spices, and plenty of eggs and butter to keep it dense and delicious. Stock up on these warm baking spices, which will keep for months if stored properly (see page 9). You could also sprinkle pumpkin seeds or add a swirl of whipped cream cheese to the top. But sometimes, I just crave the classic, perfect for nibbling alongside a warm mug of coffee.*

# spiced pumpkin bread

1 cup (8 oz/250 g) unsalted butter, melted and cooled

1 cup (7 oz/220 g) firmly packed brown sugar

4 large eggs

1 can (15 oz/470 g) pure pumpkin (not pumpkin pie filling)

1 teaspoon pure vanilla extract

1½ cups (7½ oz/235 g) all-purpose flour

1 teaspoon baking soda

1 teaspoon baking powder

½ teaspoon salt

2 teaspoons ground cinnamon

1 teaspoon ground ginger

¼ teaspoon ground cloves

¼ teaspoon ground allspice

¼ teaspoon ground nutmeg

*makes 9 servings*

Preheat the oven to 350°F (180°C). Butter a 5-by-9-inch (13-by-23-cm) loaf pan.

In a large mixing bowl, add the butter and brown sugar and whisk to combine. Add the eggs and beat until thick and smooth. Add the pumpkin and vanilla and stir to combine.

In a separate bowl, add the flour, baking soda, baking powder, salt, cinnamon, ginger, cloves, allspice, and nutmeg and whisk to combine. Add the dry ingredients to the wet ingredients and stir just until combined, a few strokes.

Scrape the batter into the prepared pan, spreading evenly and smoothing the top. Bake until a toothpick inserted at the center comes out clean or with only a few moist crumbs attached, 1 hour and 10 minutes. Let cool in the pan.

Run a knife around the inside of the pan to loosen the sides. Placing one hand on top of the bread, invert the pan and gently ease the bread out onto a board or plate. Slice the pumpkin bread thickly and serve.

Shopping Tip: Pure pumpkin is not the same thing as "pumpkin pie filling." The cans sit right next to each other in the baking aisle. They both have cute pictures of pumpkins on them. Don't go astray.

... it's a hot mess, but also pretty much the best thing you'll ever drink.

*My friend Malavika makes amazing tea. She grates loads of fresh ginger and boils the milk, and it's a hot mess, but also pretty much the best thing you'll ever drink. This version is sweet, spicy, and worth making at home.*

## magical ginger chai

6 thin slices fresh ginger

1 cinnamon stick

10 whole cloves

10 black peppercorns

6 cardamom pods

4 bags of black tea (see note)

2 cups (16 fl oz/500 ml) milk

1/3 cup (2 1/2 oz/75 g) firmly packed brown sugar

*makes 4 servings*

In a saucepan over medium-high heat, add 4 cups (32 fl oz/1 l) water and the ginger, cinnamon, cloves, peppercorns, and cardamom. Bring to a simmer, adjust the heat to maintain, cover the pot, and simmer to let the flavors infuse, 10 minutes. Remove from the heat, add the tea bags, and cover again. Steep for 5 minutes. Remove and discard the tea bags.

Return the pot to medium-high heat. Add the milk and brown sugar. Stir until the sugar has dissolved and the chai is warmed through.

Pour the chai into a teapot or strain directly into mugs and serve warm.

Shopping Tip: What kind of tea works best? I use PG Tips, but English Breakfast or any other strong, black tea will do. You don't really need anything too expensive or exquisite. That spicy fresh ginger is going to kick out, no matter what.

*On snow days, my mom used to make us Mexican hot chocolate. A mug of hot milk, steeped with cocoa and spices, still feels incredibly comforting. Whisk a big batch for friends, or just warm up one cup for yourself (below).*

## perfect hot cocoa

6 cups (48 fl oz/1.5 l) milk

1/2 cup (1 1/2 oz/45 g) unsweetened cocoa powder

1/2 cup (3 1/2 oz/105 g) firmly packed brown sugar

1/2 teaspoon ground cinnamon

Pinch of cayenne pepper

Pinch of salt

1 teaspoon pure vanilla extract

*makes 4 servings*

In a saucepan over medium heat, add the milk, cocoa, brown sugar, cinnamon, cayenne, salt, and vanilla and whisk to combine. Stir until the sugar has dissolved and bubbles just start to form around the edges of the pan. Pour the cocoa into mugs and serve warm.

Cocoa Hacks: Just One Mug

You can easily scale back this recipe for a quick single serving. In a mug, add 2 tablespoons unsweetened cocoa powder, 2 tablespoons firmly packed brown sugar, a pinch each of cinnamon, cayenne, and salt and stir to combine. Add a splash of milk and a dash of vanilla and stir to form a paste. Fill the mug the rest of the way with milk and stir to combine. Microwave until warm, stopping and stirring every minute to make sure the milk doesn't boil over. Stir to combine and serve warm.

# index

## A

Apple-Cinnamon Crumble, 161

Arincini, 39

Arugula

Arugula Salad with Fennel & Citrus, 134

Prosciutto, Ricotta & Arugula Pizza, 55

Asparagus

Asparagus & Baby Shiitake Stir-Fry, 22

Spring Greens with Lamb, Asparagus & Fingerling Potatoes, 113

Spring Vegetable Risotto, 39

Avocados

Guacamole, 124

## B

Bacon

Bacon Mac, 46

Grilled Scallops Wrapped in Bacon, 74

Pretty Green Lentils with Bacon & Feta, 31

Roasted Brussels Sprouts with Bacon & Shallots, 28

Banana Bread, Chunky Monkey, 166

Barbecue Chicken with Bourbon-Molasses Sauce, 139

Beans

Chicken Enchiladas with Black Beans & Veggies, 94

Garbanzo Burgers with Spicy Mayo, 30

Pretty Green Lentils with Bacon & Feta, 31

Three Amigos Bean Chili, 21

Beef

Home-Style Pot Roast, 133

Korean Barbecue Lettuce Wraps, 100

Meaty Lasagne, 48

Monday-Night Meatballs, 103

Porterhouse Steak with Pan Sauce & Mash, 99

School-Night Beef Burritos, 106

Skillet Cheeseburgers, Cali Style, 104

Beets & Chard, Co-Op Quesadillas with, 25

Berries, Whipped Ricotta with, 164

Bourbon-Molasses Ribs, 139

Braised Chicken Thighs with Mushrooms & White Wine, 82

Bread, Grilled Garlic, 140

Broccoli

Broccoli, Bacon & Cheddar Frittata, 145

Retro Chicken & Broccoli Casserole, 83

Spicy Broccoli Rabe Pizza, 55

Brownies, One-Bowl, with Hazelnuts & Nutella, 152

Brussels sprouts

Roasted Brussels Sprouts with Bacon & Shallots, 28

Roasted Brussels Sprouts with Brown Butter & Hazelnuts, 28

Burgers

Garbanzo Burgers with Spicy Mayo, 30

Skillet Cheeseburgers, Cali Style, 104

Burritos

Indian Burritos, 86

School-Night Beef Burritos, 106

Butter Pecan Crispy Treats, 154

Butternut Squash Soup with Fried Sage, 16

## C

Cake

Carrot Cake with Cream Cheese Frosting, 160

Chocolate Cake with Mocha Buttercream, 157

Confetti Cupcakes, 158

Cake Batter Crispy Treats, 154

Captain's Crispy Treats, 154

Caramel

Salted Caramel Corn, 129

Salted Caramel Crispy Treats, 154

Carrot Cake with Cream Cheese Frosting, 160

Chai, Magical Ginger, 169

Cheese

Bacon Mac, 46

Chard Mac, 46

Cheese Plates, 127

Co-Op Quesadillas with Beets & Chard, 25

Fontina, Mushrooms & Thyme Pizza, 55

Lobster Mac, 46

Mac & Cheese with Garlicky Breadcrumbs, 46

Parmesan & Black Pepper Popcorn, 129

Pizza Margherita, 55

Prosciutto, Ricotta & Arugula Pizza, 55

Spicy Broccoli Rabe Pizza, 55

Truffled Mac, 46

Whipped Ricotta with Berries, 164

Chicken

Barbecue Chicken with Bourbon-Molasses Sauce, 139

Braised Chicken Thighs with Mushrooms & White Wine, 82

Chicken Enchiladas with Black Beans & Veggies, 94

Chicken Pot Pie with Puff Pastry, 85

Cowboy Chicken Salad with Cilantro-Lime Dressing, 92

Existential Ramen with Chicken & Eggs, 89

Herb Roasted Chicken, 79

Masala-Style Chicken Curry, 86

Panfried Chicken Breasts with Mustard & Capers, 80

Panfried Gnocchi with Chicken, Lemon & Thyme, 49

Pasta Tubes with Chicken, Zucchini, Peppers & Pesto, 45

Portland-Style Chicken Bento, 91

Pumpkin Chicken Curry, 88

Retro Chicken & Broccoli Casserole, 83

Chickpeas

Garbanzo Burgers with Spicy Mayo, 30

Homemade Hummus, 125

Chili, Three Amigos Bean, 21

Chocolate

Chocolate Cake with Mocha Buttercream, 157

Chunky Monkey Banana Bread, 166

Cocoa Crispy Treats, 154

Killer Chocolate Chip Cookies, 151

M&M Crispy Treats, 154

Monster Granola Bars, 155

One-Bowl Brownies with Hazelnuts
& Nutella, 152

Peanut Butter & Chocolate Crispy
Treats, 154

Perfect Hot Cocoa, 169

Chunky Monkey Banana Bread, 166

Cinnamon-Apple Crumble, 161

Cocoa Crispy Treats, 154

Cookies & Cream Treats, 154

Cookies, Killer Chocolate Chip, 151

Co-Op Quesadillas with Beets
& Chard, 25

Confetti Cupcakes, 158

Corn, Sweet, with Cream & Chile, 140

Cowboy Chicken Salad with Cilantro-
Lime Dressing, 92

Crab Cakes with Caesar Salad, 68

Crumble, Cinnamon-Apple, 161

Cucumber, Yogurt & Dill Dip, 124

Cupcakes, Confetti 158

Curries

Indian Burritos, 86

Masala-Style Chicken Curry, 86

Pumpkin Chicken Curry, 88

Thai-Style Green Curry with
Prawns, 69

### D

Deviled Eggs, 128

Dips

Guacamole, 124

Homemade Hummus, 125

Romesco with Roasted
Peppers, 125

Yogurt, Cucumber & Dill Dip, 124

### E

Eggs

Broccoli, Bacon & Cheddar
Frittata, 145

Deviled Eggs, 128

Existential Ramen with Chicken
& Eggs, 89

Ham, Leeks & Gruyère Frittata, 145

Potato, Onion & Manchego
Frittata, 145

Sriracha Fried Rice with Sunny
Eggs, 42

Zucchini, Red Pepper & Oregano
Frittata, 145

Eggplant Parm, 24

Enchiladas, Chicken, with Black Beans
& Veggies, 94

Existential Ramen with Chicken
& Eggs, 89

### F

Farro with Roasted Winter
Vegetables, 36

Fennel & Citrus, Arugula Salad with, 134

Fish

Fish Tacos with Pickled Onions
& Chipotle Sauce, 66

Grown-up Fish Sticks with Yogurt-
Dill Sauce, 65

Oregon Niçoise with Hot-Smoked
Salmon, 59

Panfried Sole with Brown Butter
& Capers, 63

Teriyaki Salmon with Wasabi
Noodles, 60

Tuna-Noodle Casserole with Capers
& Dill, 62

Frittata

Broccoli, Bacon & Cheddar, 145

Ham, Leeks & Gruyère, 145

Potato, Onion & Manchego, 145

Zucchini, Red Pepper
& Oregano, 145

Fruits See individual fruits

### G

Garbanzo Burgers with Spicy Mayo, 30

Ginger Chai, Magical, 169

Gnocchi, Panfried, with Chicken,
Lemon & Thyme, 49

Grains See also individual grains

Farro with Roasted Winter
Vegetables, 36

Quinoa with Roasted Summer
Vegetables, 35

Greek Yogurt with Mango & Honey, 164

Greens See individual greens

Grilled Garlic Bread, 140

Grilled Peaches with Mascarpone
& Almonds, 163

Grilled Scallops Wrapped in Bacon, 74

Grown-up Fish Sticks with Yogurt-Dill
Sauce, 65

Guacamole, 124

### H

Ham, Leeks & Gruyère Frittata, 145

Hazelnuts

One-Bowl Brownies with Hazelnuts
& Nutella, 152

Roasted Brussels Sprouts with
Brown Butter & Hazelnuts, 28

Herb Roasted Chicken, 79

Home-Style Pot Roast, 133

Homemade Hummus, 125

Hot Cocoa, Perfect, 169

### I

Indian Burritos, 86

Indian-Style Lamb & Peas, 117

### J

Jacket Potatoes with Fillings, 27

Jambalaya with Prawns & Andouille, 75

### K

Kale

Massaged Kale Salad with Dates
& Nuts, 15

Tortellini en Brodo with Kale, 51

Killer Chocolate Chip Cookies, 151

Korean Barbecue Lettuce Wraps, 100

### L

Lamb

Indian-Style Lamb & Peas, 117

Lamb Chops with Garlic
& Rosemary, 114

Shepherd's Pie, 116

Spring Greens with Lamb, Asparagus
& Fingerling Potatoes, 113

Lentils, Pretty Green, with Bacon
& Feta, 31

Lettuce Wraps, Korean Barbecue, 100

Lobster

Lobster Mac, 46

Lobster Roll Sliders, 72

## M

Mac & Cheese with Garlicky
  Breadcrumbs, 46
Magical Ginger Chai, 16
Mango & Honey, Greek Yogurt with, 164
Marinara, 52
Marshmallow Crispy Treats
  Butter Pecan Crispy Treats, 154
  Cake Batter Crispy Treats, 154
  Captain's Crispy Treats, 154
  Cocoa Crispy Treats, 154
  Cookies & Cream Crispy Treats, 154
  Marshmallow Crispy Treats with
    Vanilla Bean, 154
  M&M Crispy Treats, 154
  Peanut Butter & Chocolate Crispy
    Treats, 154
  Salted Caramel Crispy Treats, 154
Masala-Style Chicken Curry, 86
Mashed Potatoes, Creamy, 134
Massaged Kale Salad with Dates
  & Nuts, 15
Meatball Sub, 103
Meatballs, Monday-Night, 103
M&M Crispy Treats, 154
Mole, Turkey, with New World
  Veggies, 95
Monday-Night Meatballs, 103
Monkey Bread with Pecans, Bourbon
  & Orange, 146
Monster Granola Bars, 155
Mushrooms
  Asparagus & Baby Shiitake Stir-Fry, 22
  Braised Chicken Thighs with
    Mushrooms & White Wine, 82
  Fontina, Mushrooms & Thyme
    Pizza, 55
  Truffled Mac, 46
  Wild Mushroom Risotto, 40
  Wild Mushroom Stew with Dill
    & Paprika, 19

## N

Noodles
  Existential Ramen with Chicken
    & Eggs, 89
  Teriyaki Salmon with Wasabi
    Noodles, 60

## Nuts

  Grilled Peaches with Mascarpone
    & Almonds, 163
  Massaged Kale Salad with Dates
    & Nuts, 15
  Monkey Bread with Pecans,
    Bourbon & Orange, 146

## O

Oats
  Monster Granola Bars, 155
One-Bowl Brownies with Hazelnuts
  & Nutella, 152
Oregon Niçoise with Hot-Smoked
  Salmon, 59

## P

Panfried Chicken Breasts with Mustard
  & Capers, 80
Panfried Gnocchi with Chicken,
  Lemon & Thyme, 49
Panfried Sole with Brown Butter
  & Capers, 63
Parmesan & Black Pepper Popcorn, 129
Pasta
  Bacon Mac, 46
  Chard Mac, 46
  Lobster Mac, 46
  Mac & Cheese with Garlicky
    Breadcrumbs, 46
  Shells with Grilled Shrimp, Arugula
    & Feta, 45
  Ties with Spinach, Mushrooms
    & Artichokes, 45
  Tortellini en Brodo with Kale, 51
  Truffled Mac, 46
  Tubes with Chicken, Zucchini,
    Peppers & Pesto, 45
  Tuna-Noodle Casserole with Capers
    & Dill, 62
  Twists with Tomatoes, Olives & Fresh
    Mozzarella, 45
Peaches, Grilled, with Mascarpone
  & Almonds, 163
Peanut Butter & Chocolate Crispy
  Treats, 154
Peas
  Indian-Style Lamb & Peas, 117
  Spring Vegetable Risotto, 39
Perfect Hot Cocoa, 169

Pesto, Fresh, Roasted Pork Tenderloin
  with, 107
Pigs in Blankets, 128
Pizza
  Fontina, Mushrooms & Thyme, 55
  Margherita, 55
  Prepping pizza dough, 52
  Prosciutto, Ricotta & Arugula, 55
  Spicy Broccoli Rabe, 55
Popcorn
  Parmesan & Black Pepper
    Popcorn, 129
  Salted Caramel Corn, 129
Pork
  Bourbon-Molasses Ribs, 139
  Ham, Leeks & Gruyère Frittata, 145
  Pigs in Blankets, 128
  Roasted Pork Tenderloin with Fresh
    Pesto, 107
  Smothered Pork Chops with Sour
    Cream & Onions, 109
  Spicy Braised Sausages & Chard with
    Polenta, 110
Porterhouse Steak with Pan Sauce
  & Mash, 99
Portland-Style Chicken Bento, 91
Pot Pie, Chicken, with Puff Pastry, 85
Pot Roast, Home-Style, 133
Potatoes
  Creamy Mashed Potatoes, 134
  Jacket Potatoes with Fillings, 27
  Porterhouse Steak with Pan Sauce
    & Mash, 99
  Potato, Onion & Manchego
    Frittata, 145
  Shepherd's Pie, 116
  Spring Greens with Lamb, Asparagus
    & Fingerling Potatoes, 113
Pretty Green Lentils with Bacon
  & Feta, 31
Prosciutto, Ricotta & Arugula Pizza, 55
Pumpkin
  Spiced Pumpkin Bread, 167
  Pumpkin Chicken Curry, 88

## Q

Quesadillas, Co-Op, with Beets
  & Chard, 25
Quinoa with Roasted Summer
  Vegetables, 35

## R

Ramen, Existential, with Chicken & Eggs, 89

Retro Chicken & Broccoli Casserole, 83

Ribs, Bourbon-Molasses, 139

Rice

Jambalaya with Prawns & Andouille, 75

Sriracha Fried Rice with Sunny Eggs, 42

Risotto

Arincini, 39

Spring Vegetable Risotto, 39

Wild Mushroom Risotto, 40

Roasted Brussels Sprouts with Bacon & Shallots, 28

Roasted Brussels Sprouts with Brown Butter & Hazelnuts, 28

Roasted Pork Tenderloin with Fresh Pesto, 107

Romesco with Roasted Peppers, 125

## S

Salads

Arugula Salad with Fennel & Citrus, 134

Cowboy Chicken Salad with Cilantro-Lime Dressing, 92

Crab Cakes with Caesar Salad, 68

Massaged Kale Salad with Dates & Nuts, 15

Oregon Niçoise with Hot-Smoked Salmon, 59

Spring Greens with Lamb, Asparagus & Fingerling Potatoes, 113

Salmon

Oregon Niçoise with Hot-Smoked Salmon, 59

Teriyaki Salmon with Wasabi Noodles, 60

Salted Caramel Corn, 129

Salted Caramel Crispy Treats, 154

Sandwiches

Lobster Roll Sliders, 72

Meatball Sub, 103

Sausages

Bacon-Wrapped Sausages, 147

Jambalaya with Prawns & Andouille, 75

Pigs in Blankets, 128

Spicy Braised Sausages & Chard with Polenta, 110

Scallops, Grilled, Wrapped in Bacon, 74

School-Night Beef Burritos, 106

Shellfish *See crab; fish; lobster; scallops; shrimp*

Shepherd's Pie, 116

Shrimp

Jambalaya with Prawns & Andouille, 75

Pasta Shells with Grilled Shrimp, Arugula & Feta, 45

Thai-Style Green Curry with Prawns, 69

Vietnamese-Style Fresh Rolls with Peanut Sauce, 71

Skillet Cheeseburgers, Cali Style, 104

Smothered Pork Chops with Sour Cream & Onions, 109

Sole, Panfried, with Brown Butter & Capers, 63

Soups

Butternut Squash Soup with Fried Sage, 16

Creamy Tomato Soup & Onion Toasties, 18

Spicy Braised Sausages & Chard with Polenta, 110

Spring Greens with Lamb, Asparagus & Fingerling Potatoes, 113

Spring Vegetable Risotto, 39

Sriracha Fried Rice with Sunny Eggs, 42

Steak, Porterhouse, with Pan Sauce & Mash, 99

Stew, Wild Mushroom, with Dill & Paprika, 19

Stir-Fry, Asparagus & Baby Shiitake, 22

Sweet Corn with Cream & Chile, 140

Swiss chard

Chard Mac, 46

Co-Op Quesadillas with Beets & Chard, 25

Spicy Braised Sausages & Chard with Polenta, 110

## T

Tacos, Fish, with Pickled Onions & Chipotle Sauce, 66

Thai-Style Green Curry with Prawns, 69

Three Amigos Bean Chili, 21

Tomatoes

Creamy Tomato Soup & Onion Toasties, 18

Eggplant Parm, 24

Fish Tacos with Pickled Onions & Chipotle Sauce, 66

Marinara, 52

Pizza Margherita, 55

Pasta Twists with Tomatoes, Olives & Fresh Mozzarella, 45

Tortellini en Brodo with Kale, 51

Tortillas

Chicken Enchiladas with Black Beans & Veggies, 94

Co-Op Quesadillas with Beets & Chard, 25

Truffled Mac, 46

Tuna-Noodle Casserole with Capers & Dill, 62

Turkey Mole with New World Veggies, 95

## V

Vegetables *See also individual vegetables*

Chicken Enchiladas with Black Beans & Veggies, 94

Farro with Roasted Winter Vegetables, 36

Pasta Ties with Spinach, Mushrooms & Artichokes, 45

Quinoa with Roasted Summer Vegetables, 35

Spring Vegetable Risotto, 39

Turkey Mole with New World Veggies, 95

Zucchini, Red Pepper & Oregano Frittata, 145

Vietnamese-Style Fresh Rolls with Peanut Sauce, 71

## W

Whipped Ricotta with Berries, 164

Wild Mushroom Risotto, 40

Wild Mushroom Stew with Dill & Paprika, 19

## Y

Yogurt

Greek Yogurt with Mango & Honey, 164

Yogurt, Cucumber & Dill Dip, 124

## Z

Zucchini, Red Pepper & Oregano Frittata, 145

## about the author

Becky Duffett is a writer and editor specializing in lifestyle content, including cooking, entertainment, and parenting. For several years, she worked on the Williams-Sonoma cookbook program. An avid amateur gourmet and aspiring domestic goddess, most weekends find her dodging strollers and puppies at the farmers' market, trying to read at the bakery, or roasting big dinners for friends. She lives in San Francisco.

## about the photographer

Matt Schriock is a photographer and digital artist, specializing in fine art retouching for exhibition and publication. Permanently attached to a camera, he has an incredible eye and off-the-hip approach to capturing characters and moments. Behind a laptop, he's a master of the dark arts of Photoshop wizardry. He lives in Los Angeles.

## acknowledgments

There's nothing like writing a book to prove that you have amazing family and friends. I'm so grateful for all of the help and support I received on this project.

To Matt Schriock, for his talent, patience, and good company. Matt, you see things that none of us can. To Lauren Funk, for creating a beautiful design and spending many evenings and weekends polishing the details. Thank you both for making me look good.

To Kathryn Kilner, world-class director of marketing, and a quietly encouraging friend. To Kathryn, Annie Lindseth, and Elena Cryst for opening up their beautiful apartment to cooking smells and smoke alarms. To Karen Nguyen and Mary Zhang, the best assistant food stylists in the history of scrappy, low-budget photo shoots. To Mary Z for party planning par excellence.

To Margaux Bennett for fabulous cocktail parties. To Tricia Huerta and Anne Gomez for letting me borrow their awesome deck and fill it with smoke. To Chris Sholley and Kay Takamura for endless title brainstorms. To Kate Farrell for crispy treat consultations. To Malavika Prabhu for magical ginger tea and veggie inspiration.

To my friend and mentor Elizabeth Dougherty, for unfailingly honest advice and good judgment. To Katie Moore, for the sharpest of pencils on proofread. To Roxy Aliaga, the sassiest editor I know—thank you for the borrowed confidence. To Amy Marr, Jen Newens, and Ali Zeigler, for consultations, encouragement, and teaching me how to make beautiful cookbooks in the first place.

To my mom, who always let me bake as many chocolate chip cookies as I wanted. Thank you for tying my apron strings, and invariably cleaning up my messes. To my brother Jason, bearded hipster, target audience, and my favorite taste tester.

To Dr. Stevie Osborne, my best friend, roommate, and the cleverest whiz kid I know. Thank you for eating everything, and saying it was "quite good." Thank you for chopping onions and washing pots and pans. Thank you for always believing in me. I love you more than you love jacket potatoes with chicken curry, and that's saying something.

## how to *feed* yourself

Published by Yellow Dog Books
San Francisco, California

Copyright © 2014 Becky Duffett

Printed by CreateSpace
First printed in 2014
10 9 8 7 6 5 4 3 2 1

Library of Congress Control Number available on request.

ISBN-13: 978-0692332139
ISBN-10: 0692332138

Recipes by Becky Duffett
Photos by Matt Schriock
Design by Lauren Funk